THE GRANNY WHO STANDS ON HER HEAD

Reflections on Growing Older

Ann Richardson

Cover Design by Mirna Gilman, BooksGoSocial
Cover Drawing © Bobby Clennell

This book is dedicated to the memory of my father

whose original way of looking at the world

suffuses these pages

as it did my life

TABLE OF CONTENTS

INTRODUCTION: OLD AGE IS NOT A FOREIGN COUNTRY

Somewhere in the middle of my seventies, I realised that I liked being old.

Or, to be more accurate, I liked being old, in good health and extremely lucky. Indeed, I had liked it for years without acknowledging the fact. Yes, there were definitely some downsides, I wouldn't argue about that. But there were also huge compensations, which I really wasn't expecting. Since there are numerous books about the many physical and emotional demands of ageing – the trials of being the carer of someone you love, the experience of widowhood, the survival of life-threatening diseases, to name a few – I wanted to write a celebration of being older.

Not long ago, I was reminded of the saying, "The past is a foreign country: they do things differently there," which is the first line of the novel, *The Go -Between*, written by L. P. Hartley in 1953. I began to wonder whether it was right or not, in terms of my own past. But my thoughts quickly took a different turn. The question buzzing in my head was whether the same was true of the future, when viewed from the perspective of younger people. Do we see old age as a

completely different place, with few or no familiar handles to
provide something we might hold on to?

When I was young – pick any age up to 50 or so – I definitely
thought that the future was a foreign country. It would be
strange to me and it would be difficult to cope with. And they
would definitely "do things differently" there. I looked
around at the old people I knew and they clearly had different
interests and temperaments and felt altogether different to
me. It was not something I looked forward to.

Yes, I knew that at some point I would become an old lady,
but that in itself seemed an odd concept. Me – old? Surely
not. It was, literally, unimaginable. Best not to spend much
time thinking about it.

At the same time, I vaguely assumed that if it ever happened,
I would be a different person when I got there. I would have
the same name and the same history, of course, but there the
resemblance would end. I somehow thought that when I was
magically transformed into this strange state of old
womanhood, I would be unrecognisable. I would not be the
me I had always known. It was going to be hard – I would not
know how to navigate all the twists and turns foisted on me
by the passage of time. It would be a double learning problem
– a new me in a new landscape.

How very, very wrong could I be. Now that I am an old lady
by most measures, moving inexorably toward my 80th
birthday, I realise that old age – for me – is not another
country at all. Yes, there are aspects of my life that are

different, but I don't feel that I am wandering in a strange land. And there is a great deal that is very much the same.

Old age creeps up on us rather stealthily, even if we don't make a fuss of our birthdays. Only a few things happen fast, like retirement from your lifetime's work, although in my case, I worked freelance and work just slowly stopped coming in. But generally, it simply means a few things changing each year – the hair getting whiter, the wrinkles getting deeper and so forth. You walk a little slower, your hearing becomes slightly more difficult, sometimes you even become shorter. I could list many more such small transformations. You get used to one thing, absorb that and start getting used to another. It may even be more than one thing at a time.

Yet there are very few shocks involved, in the absence of a significant death or illness, which is another matter altogether. At the same time, other things happen too. Some are definitely negative – friends die or become much more ill. Your energy slowly diminishes, so you tend to be more homebound. Your body doesn't always do what you intend. You become more aware of your own mortality. It is a time for pondering.

But on the positive side, you may acquire grandchildren and they may become a very active and joyful part of your life. Your relationship with your adult children changes and, with luck, deepens. The same is true for friendships. Not to mention marriage. And you are almost inevitably much, much more comfortable in your own skin. You feel your true self as never before.

3

And, most important, as you get used to these changes, you realise it is the same old you dealing with them. For good or ill, there is no amazing metamorphosis. Whatever your character and personality at age 30, you will almost inevitably be the same at 60 – or 70 – and beyond. If you were an optimist when you were young, you will find yourself still an optimist later. If you had a tendency to fuss over unexpected events, you are almost certainly still fussing later. If you laughed at whatever life threw at you, you will be laughing still. It makes everything much more familiar.

I was reminded that when my mother was about 50, she declared to my father that she had decided to become an "eccentric old lady". That sounded a good ambition to me at the time, but my father laughed – "You've never been eccentric in your life", he commented accurately, "so you won't be eccentric then. You will be *you*." And he was right. She never became the least bit eccentric. She died age 91 after a spell of dementia, but a serious woman to the end.

I think this is good news, although perhaps not everyone will agree. It means that by the time you reach old age – however defined – you have lived with yourself a long time and are likely to know how to cope with your own individual ways. You 'grow into yourself' and, if anything, become 'more so'. You can relax and enjoy each day more. Yes, there are some new challenges, but they are softened by new joys. None of this is inevitable, but neither is the opposite. It is not unreasonable to hope for.

This is what this book is about.

STORIES FROM MY LIFE

"Why are those people going down into the earth?"

1959

I was 17 years old, due to start university in a few weeks – and standing at the top of the Empire State Building with a group of newly arrived African students. They were full of excitement and hope at having made it to the United States, shortly to be dispersed to their respective universities. Yet looking over New York City in all its vibrant glory, one young woman standing next to me began to weep. Timidly at first, I put my arm on hers and gently asked her why. She said she was worried that she wouldn't like America after all. In her country, it was green, there was a lot of grass and trees and it was very beautiful – the United States was so very different.

What was in the mind of such students had not occurred to me, of course. It was the beginning of a lifetime of learning to see the world from others' points of view. Fortunately, I had the good sense to ask her which university she was due to go to. The University of Iowa was her reply. I promised her there would be plenty of grass in Iowa. Her demeanour changed and she flashed a big smile. "Oh really? Thank you," she replied. I never learned how she got on.

What brought me there? The previous year, a highly charismatic black preacher named Reverend James Robinson had visited my school to tell us about his project to send American students for workcamp experience in Africa. I was immediately hooked and wanted to go. (See Independence, below.) I began to take an interest in African matters.

Looking for something to do that summer, I contacted the American Committee on Africa, an organisation devoted to fostering African-American relations, and asked if I could work there in some capacity. They happily took me on as a volunteer. I can't really remember exactly what I did for them, but it must have been low level work – typing, filing and the like. I attended daily doing this work for over two months.

And I was well rewarded when, at the very end of the summer, they invited me to help out in the process of welcoming a group of 80 or so Kenyan students to New York City. This was the first in what was to become a fairly famous 'airlift' of Kenyan students to study all over the United States, which took place over four or so years. The highly popular Kenyan politician, Tom Mboya, had come to the US, obtained the interest of key people in the project and raised sufficient finance to pay for it.

The project received a lot of media attention. It was not the first time any African students had come to study in the U.S., but it was the first time they had done so in such large numbers. And for me, looking back, their visit was the first time I had been given some responsibility, working with a young and agreeable Kenyan man as a colleague and sort-of supervisor. The students were due to stay in New York for only two or three days for a period of orientation and then travel onwards to their agreed university.

Our job was initially to register all the arriving students, taking down their background details, information on where they were due to study and a lot of practical information, such as whether they had any sources of finance and, depending on their destination, a winter coat.

And then we ferried them around New York in small groups. Expenses were closely watched from above and there was some discussion of whether they would pay for me to go up the Empire State building with the group. Fortunately for me, it was decided that I deserved a treat, after working all summer for nothing. And that is how I came to see my home city through the eyes of a group of people more or less my own age, who had never until a few days before been out of the African hinterland. Well, some of them came from Nairobi, but New York remained a world away.

They were, like all new tourists, overwhelmed by the size and noise of the city. It was not easy to take it all in.

It was a complete eye-opener. They were full of questions. I wish I could remember them all now, but I have always remembered the following: "Why are all those people going down into the earth?" It took me a minute to work out what this young man was asking me. Yes, the New York City subway system would look strange if you were used to the countryside.

And there is a completely unexpected historical footnote to this story. These airlifts continued for several years. One year later, in 1960, another student, who of course I never met, came to the US through this process and went to study in Hawaii. He fell in love with a local girl.

Their son was to become President Barack Obama.

Independence

1960

We all know that countries join together and fall apart from time to time. We also know that it is best not to be around when that happens. In June 1960, Senegal gained independence from France, as part of a large period of decolonisation. A year before, it had joined with its neighbour into the Federation of Senegal and Mali, but this union fell apart in late August 1960. I know. I was there. I had a plane to catch and I was in the wrong place. I was 18 and very scared. I suddenly felt I had made a wrong decision and I might not escape.

I had followed my dream of taking part in workcamp experience in Africa, under the aegis of what was then – and still – called Operation Crossroads Africa. Together with some thirty or so other American students, we had flown to Dakar, Senegal in June 1960. Other groups had gone to a handful of other countries in West Africa. Later, the programme spread more widely, but this was the early days.

8

My group were initially housed at the University of Dakar. The plan was that, after a week of orientation in Dakar, we would build a schoolhouse in Rufisque, a small fishing town along the Atlantic coast, together with a small contingent of African students.

And it is these students that I remember most from the experience. At the time, the University of Dakar was the sole university catering for students from French Africa and it attracted the very best. A number of the older ones had lived and studied in Paris for a period. A few had been invited to Russia or China and spent some time there. They were so much more knowledgeable about the world than we Americans that it was embarrassing. They even knew more about current American politics than we did. I particularly remember being quizzed endlessly about Caryl Chessman, who had been recently executed in California and was a cause celebre across the world. I vaguely knew who he was, but many of my group had no idea at all. We could not keep up.

Although they joined us in Rufisque, most of these African students could not see the point of spending their holidays doing hard physical labour and, one by one, they slowly returned to studying or other activities in Dakar. But I made friends with one man in particular, named Mark, then 25, who had already spent three years in Paris. He ran a jazz programme on Senegal radio and seemed very sophisticated to me. He had a French girlfriend, whose family did not let them see each other, and I had a boyfriend back home, so we often spent free time together.

Over the course of two months, our school was duly built, with the help of local tradesmen, bricklayers and surveyors, and a date was set to celebrate the achievement. It was in late August, on a Friday and we were due to fly to Paris on the following Monday, as part of our journey home. If I remember correctly, the local Minister for the Interior came and gave a speech. My friend Mark had offered to take me and a couple of other Americans to visit his home town, St Louis, an old city in the north of Senegal, for the weekend.

It was on the train to St Louis that evening that we learned of the rift between Mali and Senegal and a state of emergency was, I believe, declared. Among other things, this meant that all national transport was to be closed down. I remember wondering whether the dedication of our schoolhouse was the last official act of that short-lived Government. But much more importantly, we were in the wrong place. There would be no train back to Dakar. We needed to get there by Sunday night. I was well and truly frightened.

The next day was spent going from one Government office to another in St Louis. Mark had a relative with some connection to the city's Mayor and we started there. He explained our dilemma and everyone was sympathetic, but organising alternative transport was problematic. In the end, however, someone offered the use of a small open-backed truck plus driver, to drive us back to Dakar the next day. I have no idea what money changed hands. I simply didn't think about it at the time. Perhaps I owe my friend Mark some sizeable sum.

The distance was roughly 300 kilometres and it took us the better part of the day. The back of an open truck is not the most comfortable way to pass the hours, but we were so relieved to have it that we never argued at all. I remember at some point we had stopped and I noted that our driver had laid out his prayer mat and was praying. And I remember well that the constant African sun, from which we had no escape, was tiring.

But we got back in the end, with sufficient time to pack for the airplane. It was a dramatic end to our African experience. We flew to Paris the next day as part of our journey home. On reflection, it was a period of growing independence for numerous African countries and, for me, growing independence toward adulthood. We all learn from the process of coping with the inevitable problems arising from foreign travel.

And I never did properly see the old city of St Louis.

The future mother-in-law

1962

I suppose most of us remember the first time we met our parents-in-law to be. Most likely all properly scrubbed, dressed much more formally than normal and nervous as hell. At least that is what it was like for me. I had gone to study in London (part of the well-known 'junior year abroad' tradition in the US) and had fallen in love with a British student. At the time, we weren't even talking about marriage, but I guess we both knew we were heading vaguely in that direction. It was not 'done' to live together unmarried in those days.

In my case, there was only a mother, her husband having died roughly five years earlier. I don't know who was more nervous – me or her. I already knew that she was a difficult woman, an alcoholic and very judgemental. I don't know what she had heard about me, but being an American was not in my favour.

And she was working class of a very traditional kind. She thought that her son was getting above himself by just going to university – this is before he did a PhD and became an academic economist. I was told that she rarely approved of anyone of the opposite sex who he or his brother brought home.

But I knew I should meet her some time and I did my best. I was all of 19 years old and not prone to doing things 'correctly'. I put my long hair up, wore my best clothes and generally tried to look prim and proper. Things did not get off to a good start when, on the way there, the bus conductor, who collected fares in those days, asked, "is the young lady over 14?" as bus fares were lower in that case.

Perhaps as with people everywhere, this woman's solution to the problem of meeting me was to push the boat out – providing what she felt would be a really good spread. She didn't know that I was small and had a limited appetite. This did not bode well. After a few formalities, we were invited to eat. The meal began with a large bowl of tinned soup each, which I had to finish, of course, but meant that I had relatively little room left for anything else. She then provided a large piece of steak, which I knew she could ill afford, plus three types of potatoes – boiled, mashed and roast – the sign of a really good meal among the British working class of the time.

There were probably also some overcooked vegetables. I don't remember all the details.

I have always liked good food, but I am able to eat whatever is given to me in normal conditions. I knew perfectly well that she was trying to show that I was welcome. But it was a terrible ordeal. Just too much food at every point. And no dog available, to whom I might have quietly slipped the odd piece of meat to hide the evidence. She looked sorely disappointed when I said I could not manage the dessert that she had cooked for us.

Perhaps not surprisingly, I have little memory of the conversation. It must have been very stilted as we had no interests in common and were, in any case, very nervous. We probably talked about the weather or how I liked England, always a potential subject when I visited new English people.

What I do remember was that she had decided a good way to end the day was to go to Evensong in the local church. None of us was remotely religious, but I was happy to have something to do beyond making endless small talk. My to-be-husband thought it was funny at the time, as she would never have gone to church on her own. But we duly trooped off and made nice noises about the service afterwards.

And how did I do? Much to my surprise, I am told that she thought I was "very nice." This is in spite of being the wrong nationality, interested in studying and, worst of all, involved with her son. I had somehow passed the test.

I saw this woman only once after this visit – at the wedding of my boyfriend's brother. He did not feel there was any reason for us to meet again, especially as he saw her very little in any case. In the summer, we both went off to the US to get on with our respective degrees. We got married a year later, one week after my graduation.

About eighteen months after that initial meeting, a telegram arrived, telling us that his mother had had a heart attack, fallen down some stairs, and died.

Our future children lost one grandmother at that point.

Chapter 1: REACHING OUR 60s and 70s

Introduction

I think most of us older people seem terribly surprised to find ourselves in the category called 'old'. It starts with turning 60 or 65, the traditional markers, and many of us arrive with our shoes polished and our best clothes packed like a new arrival at secondary school. What will it be like? Will people like me? Will I manage? And some simply deny it is happening or ignore it altogether.

And, like secondary school, we generally learn to fit in. Indeed, we realise that others are more or less in the same boat, experiencing similar fears, adjustments and new pleasures. It's OK, it's normal, I know my way around. It's not an ideal analogy, as at secondary school we move on again, but it will have to do.

This chapter explores that sense of surprise that we got here at all.

Are we old?

A group of friends are talking, catching up on their lives. One, aged 71, suggests she is beginning to feel old. Her friend, aged

69, says, "No, not me – I'm not old, I'm even working part-time." Their friend, aged 75, says, "No, me neither. I feel full of energy." There is an air of triumph. But what is going on? If they aren't old, who is?

The central question is – what is this "old" that they don't feel? It is surely something to do with an image they cannot – or will not – identify with. I suspect the image dates back to our view of our grandmothers – or other older women we knew – who fully expected to be called old.

These women wore sensible shoes and 'age appropriate' clothes. They darned socks and cooked everything from scratch. They stayed at home with their knitting or went out with friends to do something sedentary, like playing bridge or bingo. They would never dream of taking an exercise class. Unless they needed money, most had never worked – and, if they had, they would have retired years before. Indeed, they had no expectation of living very long, as life expectancy was so much lower than now, perhaps 70 or 71. They were at the last stage of their lives. They felt old to us, but perhaps more importantly, they felt old to themselves.

Our generation is completely different. We play tennis, we go out on dates if we want, some of us – no one really knows how many – have sex. We wear the same sort of clothes we have always worn – of course, we don't feel old. We say "you are as old as you feel" or "age is just a number" or even "60 is the new 40" and pride ourselves on how well we keep ourselves in trim. We feel vibrant and young. Are we kidding ourselves?

People do seem to fear the thought of being – or even seeming to be – old. As is constantly noted, we live in a youth culture and everyone wants to feel they are still part of it. We can dye our hair, have facelifts – not to mention all sorts of other nips and tucks here and there – and hide our advancing years reasonably well. We are, to all intents and purposes, not 'old' to the outside eye. And so it is easy for us to declare ourselves to be far from old.

Of course, some of us do feel old. We suffer from ill health or disability, have witnessed significant deaths, perhaps nursed an ill husband, wife or friend. We are no longer able to do the things we used to do. We accept the situation and readily say we feel no longer young – or even middle aged. These are an important part of our generation, but not the focus of this book.

In truth, what is wrong with being old? Why do we feel diminished by the very thought of being put into this category? If we have passed retirement age – and for many of us, that was a long time ago – we are chronologically not exactly young. Why not come out and say so?

We have the very thing that makes us old – loads of experience of all sorts of people and situations. We have had to face – and come through – crises of one kind or another. We have seen all the stages of life and helped children and possibly grandchildren through their own difficulties. And, most of all, we have the strengthened confidence that all this experience brings. Some would say we have wisdom.

My father, who always looked young for his age, worked for an international organisation which brought him into contact with people from all over the world, including those from many countries in East Asia. He struggled to gain authority in their eyes, because of the weight they placed on age. He told me that as soon as it was appropriate, he used to mention, as casually as he could, that his children were in college – or beyond – to gain the necessary gravitas.

So some of us are happy to reveal our age and some of us will deny it to the end. The central question, in my view, is whether we feel diminished by the information or empowered by it. Can we learn to settle into our third age and actually enjoy being old?

My view is that it may not last long – who knows – but it is great being here.

How do we know when we seem old?

The question of when you are officially deemed an adult – and no longer a child – is surprisingly difficult. It seems to fall somewhere between 16 and 21, but there are many definitions, differing from one country to another and, in the US, one state to another. Are you able to get married? To drive? To join the army? To use adult health services? It is a proverbial minefield.

The converse question of when you are officially deemed to be old also varies, but generally it is somewhere between age

60 and 65, related to eligibility for a pension. When I was studying social policy, a further distinction was made between the *young* old (aged 60 to 74) and the *old* old (75 plus). Indeed, I was struck by this thought on my 75th birthday – I was now *old* old.

But the sister question – when do we begin to note that others see us as old – is much more subtle. For me, it began in the London underground. I well remember the first time it happened. I was in my early sixties and standing in the train, as part of my daily routine, thinking about nothing in particular. A young man in a seat was waving, trying to get someone's attention, I assumed behind me. But I looked behind and no one was there. My brain re-jigged the situation and I realised he was trying to get *my* attention. Why?

Of course, he was trying to offer me a seat. Me! Of all odd things to do. I was young and able and waved him away to indicate I was fine. This was the very first time I was ever aware of being labelled as 'old' and it came as a shock. And then it started to happen more often. Someone would prod me and point to a person getting up, indicating that the vacated seat was available. Or they would stand up very visibly and offer the seat there and then. On tube trains, on buses. More and more frequently.

There was one period when I had a bad back and sitting down was very painful. I turned down the frequent offers. But once someone decides you need their seat, it is very hard to dissuade them. Once or twice, I even took a seat, which I didn't want, because it was too complicated to explain my dilemma to the eager helper.

19

In my experience, women are more likely to offer a seat than men and older people more likely than younger ones. They seem, more often than not, to be foreigners, brought up with an etiquette that no longer applies so readily to hardened Londoners. I do think it is happening more often. Perhaps there are more foreigners using public transport. Or perhaps Londoners generally are becoming more aware of the issue. Even young men, lost in their own worlds, do occasionally offer. Or perhaps it is simply that I am older.

Older men sometimes get one. My husband actually needs one more than I do, because of a bad knee. If we are together, I will try to ensure he gets one, although it is difficult to persuade him to sit down if I don't.

And yet, the older I get, the more I welcome an offered seat and even sometimes try to engineer one. I must admit, it helps.

A wonderful relief to get off my feet.

Son et lumières

I was recently talking to some friends about the fact that I was writing a book about being in our later years. I may have used the word "old." One immediately alerted me to be careful never to use the word "old" – "We are *older* – not old," she insisted. This pertained both to women and to men.

This got me thinking. Everyone tiptoes around the problem of what to call older (or old) people, as if it were a kind of embarrassing condition to which we must not call too much attention. This is not confined to women, but seems to be particularly acute in their case.

Oh dear. Such a problem. Old people in the UK were for many years referred to as *old age pensioners*, often shortened to pensioners or OAPs. Any woman over 60 (or man over 65) was deemed to be an OAP, correctly as they would be drawing a state pension. Although the phrase was used descriptively, it immediately conjured up someone slightly bent over and possibly leaning on a cane, like those road signs to warn drivers to be careful of old people in the area. Pensioners were assumed to be poor, to be living quiet lives and not likely to live very long. I'm not sure when it happened, but this term seems to have gone out of style.

In the meantime, the word *senior citizen* or *seniors* became very popular in the U.S. and has been growing in Britain. Aside from the confusion with those in their last year of high school or college, both of whom were known as seniors in my day, this always had the unpleasant whiff of a euphemism to me. Who, after all, would want to be called a junior? And this is only the reverse.

As my particular generation has aged, older people are sometimes referred to as *baby-boomers* in a descriptive way. The difficulty for me is the incidental association with the word 'baby', a patronising epithet for women that has always been deeply offensive to me. Sometimes this is shortened to boomers, often seen as pejorative. And some words are used for more formal occasions, such as *person of advanced years* usually in an effort not to sound condescending. The more medical term *geriatric* and the somewhat jokey term *oldster* pop up from time to time.

We all know that there are numerous words that imply an older person, particularly a woman, is decrepit, no longer able to think and, frankly, plain. There is *old crone*, followed by *old hag*, *old bag*, *old biddy* and *old crock*. Not to mention *old dear*. Even *superannuated*, although ostensibly more respectful, is not something anyone would aspire to be. When it comes to politics, the term *blue rinse brigade* suggests a more conservative – and possibly Conservative – bent. For those who don't know, it used to be common for older women to rinse their grey hair with a blue dye, giving it a blue-ish tinge.

Just occasionally, a word can actually seem respectful of older people. Derived initially from discussions about older people in other societies, the word *elder* came into fashion, with a mild overtone of wisdom. This is not really used much in ordinary parlance. And then there are the more direct insults. My son, in his teens, referred to older people as *crumblies* or *wrinklies*. These, at least, added a bit of humour.

And finally, I can't omit my favourite. A friend tells me that years ago, the French referred to *vielles femmes* (old ladies), *très vielles femmes* (very old ladies) and *son et lumières* – the latter being the sound and light show often played onto ancient castles or monuments in rural France. I have tried to track this down to more recent usage, but alas, none of my French friends could help here.

I take it all with a bit of a laugh – there are more important things to think about.

Oh my goodness, my daughter is 52

My daughter recently turned fifty-two. Yes, fifty plus. How did that happen? I was fifty myself only a few months ago – or so it seems. When it comes to our children, time seems to work at a different pace. We do what we do, go about our business and, somewhere in the background, we vaguely know we are growing older. We tend not to notice – or, in some cases, try our best not to notice – that we are ageing, too.

But how do our children age so fast? It was only a few years ago, surely, when we were chasing them around the park or helping them to tiptoe through the minefield of adolescence. Nor that long ago that we watched them trying to find themselves in their twenties and thirties. They found a job, quit and tried again. Often the same with boyfriends or girlfriends. And that was OK. We worried, of course, but it was what they were supposed to do at that age.

But you suddenly notice they are getting even older. Settling down, setting up house with a partner or even spouse – and, heavens, even having kids themselves.

Time seems to go so fast as we age. When we were children, time seemed to stretch on forever. If it was Christmas, summer was ages and ages away. You looked forward to being the next age up – to be seven when you were six, and so forth – but didn't it take a long time to come? It seemed the natural order of things that time passed slowly and I, for one, never thought to question it.

By the time you are in your thirties and forties, time speeds up a bit, but not that much. Having children in the house keeps you so busy, you don't think about time as such. Perhaps their birthday parties seem to come around more quickly than yours ever did or you notice their friends getting taller rather quickly. But somehow there was nothing alarming about the speed of things.

I have always used the age of my children as markers for particular times – we moved house when my daughter was seven, a close friend died when my son was ten. It was easier remembering dates this way, as the years tend to merge into one another with surprising ease. In contrast, grandchildren's ages are useless as markers of time, as they move so fast from one age to another. One minute they are working out how to read and the next they are learning Mandarin. They seem to change from toddlers to teenagers in the blink of an eye.

And your friends are constantly surprised about ages. Is your son really 39? – it feels like only yesterday that we took him to university! Is that daughter already a mother? Different friends are taken aback by different information, but what they have in common is surprise at the passage of time. I tend to say, "Yes, they age, but we don't. We just stay the same."

My father used to say that he didn't mind getting old, but he couldn't bear having middle aged children. I certainly know what he meant. In many ways, it is the biggest indicator of your own age. He always said I was thirty-one, whatever age

I was after that. And there is no terminology for it. The word 'children' implies people who are young, although your children remain your children whatever age they are. We can talk about our sons and daughters, but there is no distinctive collective term for these very adult adults.

But once you accept the fact, there is something pleasing about your children getting older. Especially if they have settled into a good life and have a strong sense of themselves. There is a fair chance that they are not doing what you imagined when you were chasing them around the playground. But is it good for them? Are they happy in themselves? And they probably didn't marry exactly the person you imagined all those years ago. But are their marriages (or partnerships) strong? Are they successful as parents? Do they have close friends? These are the important issues – not the actual age that has suddenly come to your attention.

And it continues right on up. I have a friend in her mid-nineties whose children are all either retired or in the process of retiring. We agreed that that was, indeed, strange. But it is exactly what happens as we live longer and longer.

We all need to get used to it.

Thinking about our grandparents

There is something about finding ourselves old that makes us begin to think about our long gone grandparents. We had known them, perhaps, solely from the viewpoint of a child or young person and we may begin to wonder more about them, now that we have reached their august age.

Many friends have told me about how important one or another of their grandparents had been to them. More likely a grandmother, as looking after children was widely seen as 'women's work' back then. Some had been effectively brought up by their grandparents, but even when this was not the case, they had often spent a lot of time with them and learned a lot from them. Many grandmothers were associated with the smells and joys of cooking. Some even said they missed a particular grandmother hugely and thought about her constantly.

Surprising as it might sound, this was a bit of a new idea to me. Yes, I knew both my grandmothers until my late teens, but they were not an important part of my life nor a big influence. They did not teach me much, did not pay me special attention or take a real interest in what I was up to. There was not a great deal of physical affection. They were just relatives who turned up from time to time, to whom I was expected to be nice.

My grandfathers were effectively absent. One had died before I was born, but we later discovered a memoir he had written for the family, so that I got some feel of him from that. The other died when I was five and I had seen him only during the occasional summer before that.

But my two grandmothers could hardly be more different. My father's mother lived on the other side of the United States and we saw her very infrequently. It was a very big deal to take an airplane in those days, so when she did spend the time and money to travel the long distance, she tended to stay a while. Although I never heard it said out loud, it was clear that she over-stayed her welcome. My father, her first son, had always been the apple of her eye and could seemingly do no wrong. My mother was another story. She had no reluctance to criticise my mother's ways of keeping house or child-rearing – nor to verbalise many other strong opinions. Her visits were therefore periods of great family tension, not conducive to a close relationship.

But she was, to her credit, interesting. She was what people might call 'a bit of a character' and liked to flirt, on occasion, with visitors, including – quite late on – with my husband. She had long felt she should have married 'better' than she did and would readily remind us of this fact. The most memorable example was having our teeth straightened through orthodontics, which I and my siblings had all benefitted from. "If they had had that in my day..." she once opined, "none of you grandchildren would have been born!" A strange hook on which to hang the serendipity of life.

She was also highly politically involved. In the autumn of 1960 just before the Presidential election, when visiting my uncle's family in a different state, she had a heart attack and thought she was about to die (she didn't). She later said that, while contemplating her death, she was very pleased that she had already voted by what we then called 'absentee ballot.' That put a whole new spin on the term.

My mother's mother, in contrast, was much more docile. She lived closer and she was dutifully invited for Christmas and other holidays, at which she – equally dutifully – took family photographs. Unfortunately, she had few interests that I could see, aside from regular bridge games with friends and the usual concerns of a well-brought up suburban widow, such as charity and her church. There was a strong cultural and political divide between her and my parents, which made her visits also a trial. I know she was worried I would marry someone 'unsuitable', which covered almost all categories you might think of. I married only after she died, but I suspect she would not have approved.

It must be wonderful to have a grandparent as a major influence in your life. Now that I am one, I realise that it is such a special relationship. You can be very close, but without the inevitable tensions that arise within the immediate nuclear family. You gain new perspectives and ways of doing things. And you also gain a small foothold in history, if one or the other talks about their own background and life as a child.

I do sometimes wonder what my grandchildren will remember about me in fifty years' time.

"It's not fair"

My daughter, aged seven, and I were on our way to the Christmas concert that her piano teacher held every year for her pupils to play for their collective parents. "It's not fair," she argued in her very natural nervousness, "the other children have been learning for much longer and of course they can play better." I did my best to reassure her that she would do fine. Which she did.

Years passed, and we were again on our way to exactly the same occasion, but she was now age fourteen. "It's not fair..." she exclaimed, with no memory of the previous occasion, "the young kids get to play easy songs with two fingers and I have to play The Moonlight Sonata." Again, I tried to reassure her that she would do fine, which she did. But I must admit that I could not resist pointing out the earlier discussion and may have left her feeling she could not win. I am good with logic, if not always the most empathetic parent. And, from her point of view, she was right. Life did not feel fair.

"It's not fair!" – how often do we hear that from our children or grandchildren, when they are playing a game or being punished or, indeed, at any number of other points in the day? And they are right – life is very unfair.

Children can find a lot of ways to note the unfairness of life. One got more ice cream, one had longer playing with computer games, one got to stay up later. It goes on and on. And we explain that yes, it is fair and then attempt to explain why. Or perhaps we say no, it isn't, but life isn't fair and we all need to learn to live with it. Or we find some other words to move the conversation on. It's not a discussion at which anyone really wins.

My brother, then aged about 11 or 12, worked out an ingenious way to even up the score. He was usually given the responsibility to pour the children's fizzy drinks if there was an occasion with guests, while my father handled drinks for the adults. If you made some glasses look fuller by packing them with ice, he discovered, other kids would choose those glasses, thinking they were thereby getting more of the desired drink, whereas in fact they were only getting more ice. At some point, he kindly shared this secret with me and we felt very smug. Looking back, it is hard to imagine how we could ever have endowed this paltry trick with any importance at all. But we did.

Adults are also quick to note that circumstances are not fair. A young man will complain that one particular friend always gets the pretty girls, when he has no special qualities to attract them. An older woman will feel slighted when a male colleague is promoted above her, although she is clearly more talented at the job. There are, of course, numerous other circumstances on which I could draw. Sometimes, we are quick to find an explanation that assures us of our case. The girls don't really like that friend, but they like the fact he has a car. It is because the employer is prejudiced against women that he has promoted the man – or perhaps it is discrimination against older people. It is not our fault. We have many such explanations up our sleeves, sometimes correctly.

My own view is that life is unfair in so many ways that it is hard to count. And why am I writing about this here? Put simply, growing older brings these out one by one, until you lose track of any sense of fairness. It is a driving force of much of our lives.

Most visibly, there is good health. Some people seem to be born with a strong constitution and the ability to fight off whatever diseases afflict them. Others fall at the first hurdle, dying young from unexpected cancer or other disease affecting young people. Or, indeed, they die horribly in a car accident, as did my younger sister not yet out of her twenties. As we age, our bodies test us constantly and sometimes, the heart or a kidney or a lung or even an innocent-looking nerve gone rogue gets the upper hand. We are left unable to lead a full life or, perhaps, disabled by pain. This is clearly not fair.

But health is only the beginning. Where most people seek the warmth and happiness of marriage or close partnership, this seems to elude some of us to the end. How much pain is represented in the statistics of divorce – the marriage ended due to a constantly roving eye or alcoholism or downright boredom. It is total luck, in my view, that the hopes of some young bridegrooms come roughly true while others fall by the wayside because these contingencies could not remotely be foreseen. The same for brides too, of course.

And then there are the children, and subsequent grandchildren, who get themselves born - or not. I did not know it beforehand – I thought naively that the interests and personalities of your children were roughly predictable. How wrong could I have been? Some seem to come out of the womb ready to please, to fit in, to make a good life for themselves. Others are very different, making life difficult for everyone around them and, most of all, for themselves. It is certainly not fair, one way or the other.

Life's rich tapestry is not rich in the same way for one and all. Most of us struggle along as best we can and feel pleased when something works out. Some like to think that any

31

success was due to their own talent and hard work. And they may be right. But having those very skills – the talent, resourcefulness and perseverance that helped them along their way – must be seen as luck in the first place. They might have been born differently. Not to mention the many little leg-ups that greeted them here and there over the course of their lives.

And should your friend feel smug and declare that his good health is down to the fact that he always ate healthy food, never smoked and took lots of exercise, you can readily agree. But also ask what qualities did he have deep within him that provided the disposition to pursue that course. It still comes back to luck, in my view.

We can have good luck or bad or, for that matter, in-between. Basically, life is just unfair. There is little more that can be said. I can only offer the phrase that French parents seem to offer their children, when asked a difficult question – *"C'est comme ça"* (that's the way it is).

I always thought that is not much of an explanation of anything, but it will have to do.

STORIES FROM MY LIFE

"Were you born around here?"

1970

After staying in the US for six years, while my English husband studied for a PhD., we moved back to England when he got an academic job in London. He had long wanted to return home and I was very open to the move, having liked living here for one brief year.

Not long after our return, we had become the proud parents of a baby girl and I was looking for something to do part-time. By chance, I found work as a junior research assistant, interviewing people with a set questionnaire. It was my first job in my new country and I was quite excited at the idea of meeting new kinds of people and talking about their lives.

These days, no research organisation would allow a young woman, still in her twenties, to wander around large council estates on her own, knocking on doors and going inside. But no one thought to worry about any potential danger and, while I had the occasional moment, I didn't worry either. The people I met were almost always friendly, happy to talk and even provide a cup of tea. The fact that I was an American undoubtedly made it more interesting for them.

Unfortunately, the study on which I was engaged was not the most exciting. Its organiser was a university professor interested in organisational behaviour and had chosen housing maintenance as an example. His main focus of study was, of all unlikely areas, the maintenance of family housing in the armed services, but he had chosen council housing as a possibly interesting comparison. In addition to interviewing those providing such maintenance, he wanted to obtain the views of tenants.

So, with his help, I had created a questionnaire about tenants' experience of housing maintenance, chose two estates in Hackney, then a very working class area of central London, and went about the process of knocking on every fifth door (or whatever system we had developed to create a random sample). Often there was no one at home, occasionally my survey was refused, but more often than not, the door was opened and I was invited in.

The questionnaire was generally very dull, but I went about it as methodically as I could. At the very end, as was common with formal questionnaires, there were questions about the person being interviewed, such as their age, plus a lot of details I can't now remember but the final one was about their nationality. It was expected that most were local British, but this was an opportunity to identify any immigrants. Research on ethnicity was then in its infancy.

By the end of the questionnaire, I was more than a little bored and was sophisticated enough, so I thought, to recognise their nationality. Against all research rules, which no one had thought to teach me, I created my own form of words to get the necessary information. I asked, very simply, "Were you born around here?"

It is from this simple question that I learned the most in the course of the whole exercise. The answer was usually yes, or occasionally no, where a woman had married a local man but came from the North of England. But now and again, I would get an answer that stopped me in my tracks. One man, with a twinkle in his eye responded, "Oh no, love, I was born across the water." My mind peddled suddenly fast – he was clearly not American, so he didn't mean the Atlantic Ocean, and he was clearly not French, so he didn't mean the English Channel. Aha, of course, he must be Irish, I said to myself, and asked accordingly. He laughed. "Oh no, dear, I'm from Bermondsey," which was across the Thames. I later learned that this is a common expression among working class Londoners. (I should add that saying "love" and "dear" to total strangers was – and still is – also common.)

But best of all was the woman who responded to my question of whether she was born "around here" by getting out of her seat and going to the window. "Come here, dear," she said, pointing down to an intersection. She noted the main road: "That," she said, "is Hoxton High Street." OK, I thought. "I was born over there on the other side, past those houses and the pub – not around here. It's very different there." I was dumbfounded at all the assumptions I needed to undo. What could I say?

You can learn a lot by asking questions.

Ancient Hospitality

1975

We were on vacation in Italy with our small daughter, visiting Italian friends, who had a toddler aged two. With no special aim, we had gone for a drive around the wilder parts of Tuscany, and found ourselves somewhere between Barga, where we had rented a house, and the Ligurian Sea. It had suddenly got late – well past lunchtime – and we were seriously hungry. Not to mention needing to pee. It was a rural area, with few restaurants at all and, in any case, Italian traditions meant there were strict timetables for mealtimes. Although this was over forty years ago, I strongly suspect that it would be unchanged in this part of Italy today.

Our friend was driving and chose to take a turn onto an unpaved road up a hill. It didn't look like a road that would take us anywhere with food. I sat in the backseat and tried to not worry about my hunger or that of the children. It turned out to be less of a hill than a mountain. Twists and turns and beautiful views. The road came to an end at the top. There was a barren place to park the car, a few houses in the distance and dirt paths leading in various directions. Not much else.

We got out to stretch and I wondered what would happen now. The two men walked off to deal with their call of nature and I watched the children, trying not to think too much about my own needs in that department. But the Italian wife strode off in search of possible food. I thought this must be a fool's errand, as there were clearly no restaurants in this remote place.

But after a few minutes, she returned with a smile, saying "There are two restaurants here." I was completely astonished and even wondered whether she was joking. She suggested that we go to the closest one and we all set off behind her on the grassy path. The views were breath-taking. We were very high, indeed. I later learned we were 950 metres above sea level.

We arrived at an ordinary house and a woman came to the door, welcoming us and encouraging us to enter. She talked with our friends in fast Italian (I could understand the occasional word), telling them she could prepare some pasta, eggs and ham – would that be suitable? It was, of course, a wonderful offer at that point.

We were taken into a room with a long table and hams and salamis hanging from the ceiling. She bustled around and went off to the kitchen to prepare the food on a wood fire. We women were able to use her toilet and she served us in good time. I wish I could say that it was the best meal I have ever eaten, but that would not be true. But it was fine – and completely amazing to be there at all. Washed down, of course, with some local wine. And when we were finished, she asked a fair price, but by no means a notably low one.

As we walked back to our car, I asked my friend what was going on. Why was a local woman so ready to feed a group of six foreigners on the spur of the moment? She said that for centuries, pilgrims and travellers of all kinds would walk from place to place and naturally need somewhere to eat and sleep. And there were always people ready to accommodate them, known to everyone in the area, so they could be suitably directed.

What we had chanced upon was a remnant of this long almost-lost tradition. It was truly memorable to be part of it. And we had only driven up a steep hill.

Much later, I wrote to my Italian friend to ask if she knew where we had been, as there were certainly no signposts. She said it was San Pellegrinetto (which means 'little pilgrim') in the province of Lucca. I looked it up on Google. Its current population seems to be 34.

Almost medieval.

Meryl Streep and Me

1976

The form letter came as a complete surprise. As an American living in London, I had joined Democrats Abroad as a way of keeping in touch with my origins and perhaps meeting some like-minded people. In fact, my membership was perfunctory and I never went to any meeting.

The letter informed me that a film company was looking for American extras for a film being made just outside London and would I like to attend an audition? An amusing idea, I thought, but not for me. I was busy with work, as well as looking after my seven-year-old daughter. I had no need to be an extra. I certainly didn't want to be auditioned, which sounded scary. I threw the invitation into the bin.

But my family had other ideas. I told them over dinner that I had been invited and both husband and daughter immediately became very insistent. "You've got to do it." I demurred. They pressed. I went to my study wastebasket and pulled out the crumpled invitation. They did not let up. Go, it won't be anything to worry about. I went.

And so it happened. The 'audition' consisted of sitting in a school auditorium, with a brief introduction about why we were there, including the assertion that Americans would 'look' more American than English people would. A woman then walked up and down the aisles pointing at one or another of us, saying yes we were wanted or no, we weren't. I was wanted. I never knew why.

I was fortunate that my work as a junior researcher was part-time and very flexible, so it was easy for me to take a few days off. The work would take place over two or three days, with a bus on hand to take us to the studio in the outskirts of London. My husband would get my daughter to school and back.

And this is how I came to be an extra in the film Julia, starring Jane Fonda, Vanessa Redgrave and Jason Robards, directed by Fred Zinnemann. It was about the American playwright,

Lillian Hellman, and her attempt to smuggle cash into pre-war Germany at the request of her Jewish friend Julia. Not that I knew much of that at the time.

We extras were used for several scenes, but my moment of glory took place in only one – an after opening night dinner at Sardi's, *the* place that theatre people went on such occasions. It was famous for its cartoons of theatre people all over the walls. (I was taken there years later by my parents, just to see how it looked in real life. It was not very different from the film set. Having opened in 1921, it still exists one hundred years later.)

We were all dressed in costumes of the period, plus a wig and make-up, so I looked nothing like my normal self (short hair and no make-up). I was amazed by the detailed trouble taken over people who would only be in the background. Someone kindly took a picture and posted it to me (this was long before smart phones). A friend once saw it and commented, "You could be quite pretty with long hair." So much for me.

What is it like to be an extra? I soon found that it was very boring most of the day. We spent a lot of time sitting around reading or chatting amongst ourselves. In addition to the London Americans, there were some American extras who had flown over with the cast and a few other English ones. We were all intermingled and I learned from the experienced extras that we should hope that the filming went on for a long time, because we would then be paid overtime.

On set, it became more interesting. We were seated at tables with food in front of us and warned not to touch it. There was real shrimp cocktail, but they would not vouch for its freshness or safety. When filming began, we had to look like we were in conversation, which was not too difficult as we had been talking all day. But we could watch the actors surreptitiously, of course, as well as the director.

In addition to the filming, I remember two things about those two or three days. First, I was disappointed with myself for not approaching Jane Fonda, who at one point was about three feet away from me waiting to go on. I had known Tom Hayden, her then husband, at university some years before and I would have liked to pass on hello. I decided it would be inappropriate for me to interrupt her while she was 'in character' and the moment was gone.

Second, I watched a scene being filmed, where Jane Fonda was talking to a young somewhat awkward actress with the peculiar name of Meryl Streep. She looked extremely uncomfortable and, I thought, with her apparent lack of ability and her odd name, she would not go far. I even remember wanting to put an arm around her – she was only six years younger than me, but I felt motherly – and give her some sort of comfort.

So much for my perspicacity. Although I did read subsequently that she said it was her first film and she definitely did feel uncomfortable.

I saw Julia, of course, when it came out – and on the television years later, when I could stop and rewind. There was no sign of me whatsoever – just a blur as the camera panned from one end of Sardi's to the other at the moment that Lilian Hellman (Jane Fonda) made her grand entrance. It was not a terrible film, but not a great one either and seems to have disappeared into the mists of time.

The beginning and end of my film career. I don't need to tell anyone that Meryl Streep went on to impress the world, including me, with her sensitivity and skill as one of the foremost actors of our time.

One should cut a little slack to first films, first books and first everything else.

Chapter 2: YES, SOME THINGS DETERIORATE

Introduction

I suspect the first thing that anyone thinks when they hear the term 'old age' involves some form of decrepitude. "Do come meet my elderly friend," your friend says, and you imagine someone doddery, if not completely disabled. He or she will look old and wrinkly, will probably be grumpy and it will be hard to find it a pleasant occasion. It was always thus.

Yes, however much we older people enjoy our lives, the situation has a bad rap. And there is some reason for this fact. Our bodies do age – no getting around it – and our health is generally not what it was. Our energy diminishes, so we cannot get as much done in a day as we did once. And we are often surrounded by an air of loss – of friends who have died, of houses we have left and an awareness of our own impending mortality.

It will be clear that I think old age has much more to offer than this picture, but I want to start by addressing it head on.

Ageing Bodies

When my son, now in his late thirties, was about five years old, he made a remark that has stayed with me ever since. He had gone through a stage, thankfully brief, when he would pee unexpectedly, leaving a small visible stain on his dark grey school trousers. At some point, I asked him, probably with some exasperation, couldn't he tell when it was coming? "No, Mum," he said, "it is kind of like an ambush."

He hit the nail on the head. There is no control. It starts as early as any of us can remember – we ran too fast on a pavement, we climbed that tree and, all of a sudden, we found ourselves on the ground and in pain. From small scrapes to broken limbs, we learned early on that our bodies could be a nuisance and did not behave as we had planned.

Not to mention the many childhood diseases. I got absolutely all of them – measles, German measles, even scarlet fever, which was very serious in those days. I have a number of chicken pox scars to remind me of that particular bout. And, of course, numerous colds and flus that came and went, as I mixed with other children at school.

Our teens and beyond brought an even bigger ambush – the menstrual period. Over time, it arrived when we least wanted it and, for some of us, on no particular schedule. We waited for it to come and, at some point, worried when it did not. Or, we wanted children and worried when it did. We women have all spent some hours over the course of our lives thinking about what was or was not happening down there. With no control.

Of course, as we grew older, we were subject to large numbers of potential illnesses. Many of us have been through one or more life-threatening diseases and many of us have lost friends through this route. Cancer is the obvious culprit, but there are plenty more. I lost a very good friend to the last pandemic of our time, AIDS, back when it was still a killer. And now, many of us will have known someone who contracted Covid-19.

But things only get worse as we age. "Old age is not for sissies," they say, and they are right. We cannot hear or see as well as we used to, we can no longer run as fast as we would like, if we can run at all. We become more prone to serious illnesses that stop us in our tracks. Diseases we have heard of and diseases we have never heard of and could never have imagined. And even the problem with which I began, suffered then by my then five-year-old son, rears its annoying head.

And for some of us, although presumably not those reading here, we lose our minds, bit by bit to some kind of dementia. This is an ambush like no other – not part of anyone's life plan.

I don't know how others feel about all these events taking place within their own bodies. Do they quietly accept that this is part of being human and do their best to struggle through with dignity? Some undoubtedly feel it is part of God's plan.

Not me. I get very incensed and rail against them. I have been amazingly healthy all my life, as was my father before me. And, like him, I get enormously angry when my body lets me down. How dare it not do what I want it to? Who gave it permission to succumb to a cold or flu or worse?

Yes, I know this makes no sense. I should accept each challenge as it arises. It is an expected part of life. Others are doubtless made of stronger stuff. My husband says I will be indignant on my death bed – and it may well be true.

I will let everyone know if he was right.

A loss of energy

For all of my life, I have felt out of sync with many of the assumptions of popular culture. A strong one is that the time people look forward to most is when they have finished work and can let their hair down. This may be on a day-to-day basis, so that the high point is when they leave their workplace and 'go for a pint' down at the pub or, for others, have a glass or two at the wine bar. And in the course of the year, the high point is the summer holiday when you leave the day-to-day work behind and can finally lie down at the beach. Anything connected to 'work' is to be avoided as much as possible.

I am not so sure. I know a lot of people – and I am certainly one – who are much more driven by the desire to be doing something. And, preferably, something of value to someone. Doing nothing can certainly be pleasurable for a while. But its main use, to those of us with this mind-set, is to ensure that your brain or body is well rested, so that you will be firing on all cylinders when you return to purposeful activity. It is not an end in itself.

There are, of course, a myriad of ways to be 'useful'. Some are carers for someone else and need to engage in a whole range of activities to meet their needs. Others may like building things from scratch or taking them apart in order to understand them. And some may simply want to get things done around the house – clean out that cupboard or make those new curtains. Alternatively, like me, some like to engage in creative activity, whether writing books or painting pictures or inventing new recipes in the kitchen. And much, much more.

We may or may not do these things well. We may or may not be satisfied with the result. But the key point is that the activity is important to us and helps us to feel that our time was well spent. We would rather do them than laze around.

What makes us so clearly one way or the other? I was brought up by a mother with a ferocious work ethic. She was in any case unusual in having worked in a professional job while bringing up three children in the 1940s and '50s (no surprise now, but then it was distinctly unusual). She was not keen on 'relaxation', although she would read at times and, in the summer, liked to weed her garden for this purpose. Perhaps I get it from her.

If we are in any way moulded by our schooling, then that, too, pushed in the same direction. I went to a very academic girl's private school in New York City, whose motto was "in truth and toil" and whose mascot was a beaver. Might one detect a strong work ethic here? Perhaps hard work was imprinted onto my brain by a daily dose of toil.

But I do wonder. If I had been born with a penchant for taking it easy, I might have rebelled heavily against such influences. As I watched my two very different children grow into adults, I increasingly questioned the impact of nurture in comparison to nature. I think we come out of the womb with a lot of characteristics that we spend a lifetime discovering. But they were there, just as much as the tilt of our nose or the colour of our hair.

But whatever the cause, one sad discovery about growing older is that we tend to get tired more easily. We lose the resilience we had when younger and our batteries run down faster and faster. This starts at different ages for different people, but seems to creep up on us when we are not looking. As far as I can see, it increases slowly each year and greatly diminishes our energy for getting things done.

For those of us with an eagerness to be engaged in positive activity, this lack of energy is incredibly annoying. It means we can't work for long periods without becoming tired. And the definition of that 'long period' slowly shortens from a day to half a day to even an hour.

Our body becomes a battleground – our head wants to get something done, but our body rebels. That old saying "The spirit is willing, but the flesh is weak" comes into play. At the end of a day, we find ourselves disappointed with the paltry amount accomplished. We had such great plans, but we got little or nothing done.

It is not so different from the Covid-related lockdowns we have suffered in the UK and others have done elsewhere.

They are a kind of imprisonment where we cannot do what we want, what one of my grandsons called "being under house arrest."

A lack of energy is close enough to house arrest.

The irregular memory

Conversations with my husband often go something like this:

"I saw that nice guy just now in the supermarket and said hello."
"What guy?"
"You know, the one we met last summer on a boat – he was tall and very nice. He had a wife with red hair and I think there was a small dog."
"Oh, yes, *that* guy. He was very nice. Are they living near here now?"

Or

"Shall we go see that film that is on down the road?"
"What film?"
"You know, the one that was made by the same guy as that terrific film that made us laugh out loud."
"Oh, yes, good idea. What time is it on?"

How many conversations take place among older couples that sound something like that? Never a name in sight – or any that really help. Anyone from outside would be baffled. Yet we often know what we are talking about. These conversations can be annoying, as we don't always get the connection we want. And they can, of course, go on a lot longer, but this seems enough to demonstrate the idea.

But they are not the real problem. What really bothers me is when I can't remember the really important facts that I should have at my fingertips. I am not talking about who was President in 1953 or what is the capital of Switzerland. No, it is all those little personal facts that you ought to remember, but can't. And it can get you into trouble if you aren't careful.

When we were younger, my friends had husbands and children and you could generally remember their names. I had met them, after all, and knew something about them. I could picture them in my mind. But now they have grandchildren who I've never met. They've talked loads about them, of course, but my memory isn't what it was and I lack the visual framework. It is so hard to keep up. How many grandchildren did they have? From their son or their daughter? And wasn't there one with a problem, but which one and what was the issue?

You meet for the occasional chat and try to re-make contact. Didn't this friend have a daughter with twin boys? Or was that someone else? Were they born a long time ago or are they still small? Time goes so fast, they are probably older than I think.

Well, I can usually find a way of saying "I'm sorry, but I can't remember the names of your grandchildren", which gives leeway for them to offer number, age and gender. And which child had what grandchildren when. Sorting that out will get you back on track.

But there is more. Take their grown-up children, whose lives I have heard a lot about over the years, but I haven't seen them for ages. Sometimes, there is a vague memory that there was some problem in the past that I was told about. Was there a son with a messy marital problem – did they get divorced or sort it out? Or was it the daughter? I should know, but it has completely gone from my head.

Or was it a work problem? Did the daughter get fired or made redundant? Little details can be very important. It looks thoughtless to have forgotten. Perhaps I can get by with "How is that son of yours getting on?" and hope that covers all contingencies. With luck, I won't have to reveal my forgetfulness.

But then comes the killer. We might be friends with an older couple who we don't see often, and I can't for the life of me remember whose parents are still alive. I can't say "How's your father doing?" if he died two years ago in difficult circumstances, which they told me all about. But I also don't want to offer condolences if the man is in rude health.

Two people means four parents. Oh dear. And this does matter to people. It's not like the names of grandchildren. This happens more often than I want to think. I've never found a good solution, aside from keeping the conversation going long enough and hoping it comes up naturally.

Sometimes, a friend will say "After my father died…." And I breathe a big sigh of relief.

One should really keep a notebook for all such information – little lists of children, grandchildren and what they are all up to. And definitely the deaths of parents. It would make conversations a whole lot easier.

Perhaps my friends have the same problem.

Giving up driving

Not that long ago, the late HRH Prince Philip, the Duke of Edinburgh, in his late nineties, was in the news in the UK. He had had a car accident – the car he was driving had ended up on its side – and it was reported that he was a bit "shaken up." As you would be, even if you were half his age.

It started some conversations about old people and driving. This is a serious issue – and one which affects a lot of us these days. In my case, it was my father. I lived an ocean away from my parents and kept in touch by telephone, but went to visit a couple of times a year or more. My dad would always meet me at the airport – with his car, of course. At some point, when he was in his mid-eighties and his eyesight was failing, I began to worry for his safety. And that of other people with him, including myself.

He had always been an excellent driver and never travelled far. Mostly, he drove around his quiet suburban neighbourhood. Indeed, he often ferried other residents of his retirement community around the area for shopping or other outings. This was much appreciated and he enjoyed that fact. Not surprisingly, he also loved the sense of freedom that owning and driving a car brought.

So, it was a hard subject to broach. "Don't bother to meet me at the airport," I said breezily a few days before I was due to travel. But he wasn't fooled. "You're worried about my driving," he replied cannily, "but really I'm just fine." I asked him to get his friend, who was a lot younger, to drive him to the airport. Which he did.

Later, I raised the subject again. I stressed that I was worried because of his eyes. He had age-related macular degeneration and didn't really see that well. I noted that there might be a small child in front of the car. Without missing a beat, but with a slight smile, he answered, "Perhaps – but there probably won't be."

But he knew he was beaten. He knew himself that he shouldn't be driving. But he had loved his car for as long as I could remember – indeed, from before I was born. And now, in his old age, it gave him independence and a role in helping others.

As we know, stopping driving for old people is not mainly about the car. It is also a symbol of decline and loss of faculties. It tells you that you are on the way down. But he did decide to stop. Perhaps he was relieved, but he never indicated any such emotion. And at dinner, a number of his friends – who had already been told of my audacity – thanked me. They had tried hints, they had tried reason, but he wouldn't listen. At last, he had listened to me.

This is clearly a problem all over the world. Soon after this happened, I spoke to a friend in Germany and she had had the same problem with her father. Another friend in the UK had it with her mother. This was a universal problem – how to tell an otherwise independent parent that they should stop driving. You are embarrassed, they are defensive – and it is altogether difficult for everyone.

And as we age, we face this issue with respect to ourselves. We love our cars, we love the freedom they bring and it is easy to convince ourselves that our minor frailties have not grown too large for us to cope. I am in the unusual position of never having owned a car. Or to be accurate, never in the last fifty plus years. It had been convenient where we lived then, but we moved to New York City, where a car was definitely inconvenient and, moreover, unnecessary. When we moved to London, we were so used to living without a car, it made sense not to. We took taxis frequently and hired a car as needed on holiday.

This was altogether a good choice, but it had one side effect I never thought about. My husband having never learned to drive, I did all the driving when it was called for. But this did not add up to much – at most two weeks a year and often less. As I grew older and less certain of my reactions in any emergency, I concluded earlier than most that it would be best for me not to drive. This has affected our choice of holiday and is disappointing for that reason, but I feel safer as a result.

But let me finish my story. Immediately after that trip from the airport when my dad was not driving for the first time, I found a bowl of flowers on the table in my room. This was very unusual and I was taken aback. With them, he had left a note – "With love and forgiveness." Later, I asked him, of course, what he was forgiving me for. "For telling me not to drive," he said.

We all do things in our own way.

Downsizing

There was a brief period a few years ago when my husband and I thought we should downsize. Our large and comfortable old house, the desired choice when the children were small, was perhaps more than we could manage. As a lot of repairs were needed and seemed to multiply every year, It seemed the sensible decision. We signed up with a number of estate agents and went to see half a dozen properties or so, some terrible but some perfectly nice. We even – almost – made an offer on one. And then one of us said yes, we could move there, but it wouldn't be as nice or as comfortable as where we are. Why move? And the whole project came to a halt.

When I was young, I would look at old people living in big houses and think it was all wrong. Young families needed their space, so why didn't they just move on and let others have their houses? And anyway, wouldn't they prefer a place that was easier to manage? Ah, yes. If only it were that simple. As we of older years well know, moving anywhere is a very major decision and a very difficult one. Perhaps some find it easy, but I have yet to meet them. It is a huge upheaval, both practically and – much more importantly – emotionally.

Downsizing means finding a new place to live. So many questions. Do you move to a new area to be near your children or simply to gain new experiences? But that means leaving behind all your local knowledge, such as the doctor you have trusted for years and the best shops for your favourite food. And you may well miss the neighbours – the people who look after the cat when you are away or even help out when you are ill. Such support is not easily or quickly replaced.

There is also the question of what kind of house or flat you move on to. You expect it to be better, but you also know there may be hidden problems. You may find you miss having that extra room. Or the walls are too thin and the neighbours noisy. Or perhaps it is harder to get around by public transport.

But most difficult of all, downsizing means sorting through all your things and throwing – or giving – a lot away. To young people, such sorting may seem like nothing more than a lot of boring afternoons spent going through old stuff. To us, in contrast, it means confronting some heavy emotional issues. Many of the things we own have a significance for one reason or another. Some remind us of our childhood or middle years. Some belonged to our parents or even grandparents. Going through these things means thinking about our lives and what was important in them. Getting rid of them means saying good-bye to our past. These are difficult tasks, indeed.

Of course, there are many good reasons to move. Those of us lucky enough to own a large house will find they can release some equity, providing a tidy sum for doing something nice or simply helping the next generation. A smaller place will also be cheaper to run and easier to clean and maintain. It may be newer, brighter and altogether more cheerful. Heaven only knows, we can all walk around our old and lived-in houses and see so many areas needing improvement – the tired carpet, the chipped tiles, the rather worn wallpaper.

All in all, it is a very difficult decision. We want to act when we are young enough to weather the upheaval. And we certainly don't want to be faced with a move just after a spouse or partner has died. Not to mention when we find ourselves ill or incapacitated. A lot of us will conclude – like us – that it is an excellent idea to move on, but maybe it could wait a few more years.

There are probably a lot of us with our heads in the sand.

Being condescended to

You can learn a lot from children. When my son was not yet three, I realised he had a quality I had never seen in any other children of my acquaintance. It took some watching and some thinking, but I finally got it pinned down. He simply did not accept child status. As far as he was concerned, he was not less equal than the larger people he came into contact with – whether parents, childminders, teachers, our friends or anyone else. Yes, he needed to learn from them (when he wanted to) and yes, they would insist on bossing him about, but somehow, in his mind, he was their equal.

This underlay a large number of his interactions as he went about the process of growing up. It was never easy – for him or the rest of us. As a young child, he loved collecting facts of all kinds and had a good memory for them. Even at the age of five, he had no problem correcting teachers when their facts were incorrect. Nor us, of course. It was more than the 'terrible twos', where children want to do the opposite of what they are told for the sake of it. Nor was it the natural ebullience of a normal boy. It was a complete mindset that coloured his response to the world in which he found himself.

I tried to explain this to my friends. If we found ourselves on another planet, for example, we would soon realise that we needed to learn the language, the customs, the history and the belief systems of the local people – BUT we would be darned if we would be talked down to. We were their equals – we just had a lot to learn. Why shouldn't a small child feel the same way?

I found this mindset fascinating. In my own childhood, it would never have occurred to me to question my status as a less-than-adult person, i.e. a child, and therefore a somewhat lesser being. It made me very conscious of the many ways in which we condescend to children.

I hadn't thought a lot about this quality until very recently when I realised – or perhaps I should say remembered – that there is an even worse tendency to condescend to the old. There is something about a lot of wrinkles that brings out a wish to talk down. This is exacerbated when the old person has the bad luck to be in a position of dependency, such as being hospitalised. The "how are we today, Ann?" asked in a high voice, is not something I look forward to.

Luckily, this condescension has not entered my life – or that of friends – very much to date. Perhaps we don't look decrepit enough. But my husband was approached recently by a young researcher, doing a study on the frail elderly and clearly keen to approach all such people with the right attitude. Yet once you have the need for an 'attitude' instead of a normal interaction with another human being, the trouble begins.

Her concern was to determine whether he was frail enough for the study, asking questions in such a way to suggest she thought he was probably a bit dim. This did not go down well. He, being a former academic, was trying to get her to define her terms. In the end, she decided he was not frail enough, which I am sure was right, but the whole experience did not leave a good taste in his mouth.

This wish to condescend to old people, when you think about it, is very odd. We are the people who have seen so much more of life, have handled so many more difficult situations. Yes, if we have lost our bearings through a diagnosis of dementia, that may be a different matter (although even then, the usefulness can be questioned), but otherwise, where does it come from?

I hope I never find out.

The loss of friends

Roughly twenty years ago, I was chatting to a very reflective friend of my parents, living in the same retirement community and aged 96. My father had just died and I thought I had run up a large phone bill talking to his friends about the event as well as phoning home to talk to my family. She said, anyone should consider themselves lucky to have a high phone bill. At her time of life, she said, her phone bills were very low, because she had so few friends left to talk to. That brought home the point very vividly.

Clearly, one of the very sad aspects of growing older is the slowly mounting deaths among friends. Each and every loss diminishes our lives a little bit more. These may be old friends we have known from childhood or someone who we just met, but had connected with and held high hopes for a lasting friendship. I guess it is just down to luck as to whether you have lost a lot of friends over your life or just a few. I have been relatively lucky in this respect, but nonetheless, they do add up.

What somehow surprises me is how many varying circumstances there are. You might think a death is a death is a death. But that is not how it is. Indeed, each one seems surprisingly different. There is the death of my friend who had been living with AIDS since I met him, about whom I have written before. He was young and that made it poignant. He would sit in my kitchen and talk about all manner of things, but more than once he just looked at me and said, "It's not so much to ask, I just want my life." And he was right. At 30, you should have a life to look forward to.

Perhaps my greatest loss was of a friend from college, who I had known for over fifty years. We had seen each other through various early boyfriends, then marriage, then children and eventually grandchildren. She was a very deep person, perhaps not surprisingly as she was a therapist, and rarely did 'small talk'. We once met for lunch when we had not seen each other for five years. I went to her office, she put on her coat and walking up the road, immediately launched into a discussion of her worries about her daughter. None of the usual "how was your flight?" which I always find boring. Who cares about my flight! She died from lung cancer, having lived a long time in its wake.

But there are the sudden unexpected deaths. I had a writer friend, to whom I wasn't close, but we enjoyed each other's company. He lived alone, had many friends and learned that he had an inoperable brain tumour and would not live for more than a few weeks. I can just envisage him wondering what to do. His solution – surprising at the time, but actually very sensitive and sensible – was to post a notice to this effect on his Facebook page. He also said "thank-you" to all his friends. This gave everyone an opportunity to write kind or thoughtful words to him while he was still alive, while I am sure his closest friends rallied around.

And there is one longstanding friend who is heading downwards as I write. She had always told me that if she got to some point when there was little to live for, she would turn her face to the wall. I argued with her at the time, but in the end she was right. As an outsider to her family, there is so little you can do.

I want them all back.

Thinking about dying

It happens more and more these days. I am cleaning up the house or on my way to the shops and I suddenly wonder what if that headache turned out to be a brain tumour and I was suddenly at death's door. Or what if my husband of so many years were to die and I would find myself suddenly alone? It may sound morbid, but in fact something of the kind will happen at some point. What would it be like? Would I cope?

I know I am not alone. We do, as we grow older, begin to think about dying now and then. Many of us prefer to think it will never happen and leave it at that. But those who like to prepare themselves for what is coming down the line are likely to give it a passing glance from time to time.

Before I was sixty, I rarely gave dying much thought at all. The possibility of my own or my husband's death seemed almost as remote as it did when I was a child, which is to say it was over a very distant horizon. Now that I am considerably older, I have to face the fact that our remaining years are increasingly limited. The statistics are not brilliant as you grow older for obvious reasons. And, with each quickly passing year, they only get worse. I don't know, of course, but it is time to begin to recognise the situation.

Yes, some of us live well into our nineties – and centenarians are becoming much more common. I even have good genes, with current good health and my parents living to age 90 and 91 respectively. Yet these are details. The truth is we will grow older and frailer and will have to face the end sooner or later. In the words of a young woman living with AIDS when it was a fatal disease, "You haven't got forever anymore."

Is it the moment of dying that we worry about? Although some people die in great distress, the much greater likelihood is that we will do so fairly peacefully. The profession of palliative care is getting increasingly clever at keeping people free of pain. In the coming years, it can only get better. I haven't reached the stage of thinking about where I would want to be when I die, although I know most people want to be at home. I just hope that I will be reasonably at peace with myself. When the time comes, I want to go gently into that good night.

Nor do I often think about my own funeral. Occasionally, when I hear a particularly beautiful piece of music, I will say casually "you can play that at my funeral." But in fact, it would be better played at a funeral I was attending during my lifetime as I would actually hear it.

Or is it the fact of no longer living that we worry about? Of no longer being there to enjoy the many pleasures of life. Or no longer being there for our family and friends, some of whom may rely on us. These are undoubtedly 'heavy' issues, which we need to prepare for.

In fact, we do make many preparations without thinking of them as such. The urge to downsize stems partly from the wish to make our passing easier for those who must administer our things after death. For those who have done this for someone else, it must come home to them how very complex such matters are. Visits to long-lost friends or relations – or those we don't see very often – may also be stimulated by the thought of doing so before it is 'too late'. Such thoughts may remain unspoken, but are nonetheless real for everyone concerned.

If anything, I think less about my own death and more about the possible death of my husband, as statistically this is the more likely first event. Having been married almost all our adult lives, it is admittedly a bit scary to think about being suddenly alone. Those who are already widowed will doubtless know much more what I mean.

Although I really am not obsessed with death, I have written two books dealing with two different aspects of it. One was about young people with HIV and AIDS in the 1990s, all of whom were dying because there then was no cure. It is not a morbid book at all, but it is an honest one about people facing an early death. I was impressed with their resilience and called it *Wise Before their Time*, because that is what I felt they were.

The second is about people who work with the dying. I had volunteered in a hospice for four years and found it fascinating that so many people could go to work each day to help people to die. I interviewed nurses, doctors, chaplains of various faiths, administrators and even a very reflective chef.

I called it *Life in a Hospice*, again because this is what it was about – the living before the dying.

Not long ago. I watched a TV interview with Sir Ian McKellen, who always struck me as a very thoughtful man. In his 80s, he said he did think about death quite often and had even planned his own funeral. And noted that he thought it sounded like such a good occasion, he wondered if he could plan an early dress rehearsal so he could attend. He surmised that old people thought about death a lot, because it was a form of preparation. When the time actually came, it probably helped them to feel that they are ready.

I think that he is exactly right.

Life ends in the middle of a sentence

I heard an expression not long ago that stopped me in my tracks. It had the ring of a famous saying, although when I investigated, it turned out not to be. But more importantly, it had some real profundity. It said, simply, "Life ends in the middle of a sentence."

Life ending in the middle of a sentence basically means that the end of life is not tidy. And, I suspect, that is right more often than it is wrong. Which made me wonder about getting my own life 'in order' ahead of time. Yes, when the end comes, as it must someday, we want to be ready. We want our things to be sorted and our children not to be left with the awful task of sorting things out.

Some people have undoubtedly met this goal already. They will have carefully downsized both where they live and what they own. In the process, they will have sorted out all those old papers, with many thrown away and the important ones carefully organised. Their books will have been sorted and cut down to a minimum. More significantly, they will have handed down all the precious memory-filled items that they wanted to ensure landed in the hands of a particular daughter or son. Or, perhaps, grandchild or, indeed, friend. They will have read through their last will and made sure it is in a safe place.

In sum, all that stuff that seems to accumulate over the years will have been substantially reduced. Everything will be in its place. The process of cleaning up after their demise will be easy. They will have left no mess behind. Congratulations are due.

But is it really that easy? Can most of us be quite so fully organised? We may have some sort of plan and a wish to do the right thing, but I question whether we can ever have such tidy lives. And, most importantly, would we wish to do so? The image of everything being in its rightful place suggests that we have had our lunch, tidied up, put the plates away and are sitting quietly in an armchair waiting for the Grim Reaper to knock on the door.

In truth, life is not like that. We all have projects of one kind or another. For me, it is writing, but for others it may be painting or knitting a special outfit for a grandchild or planning the next holiday. Or even the one after that. Human beings don't often put their feet up and wait. They get restless, they mooch around and they get themselves stuck into something that interests them.

Even if we don't have exact plans, we may well have dreams. This came home to me very vividly when I was helping my friend dying of AIDS roughly thirty years ago. We were writing a book together and had become good friends. He had lived longer than anyone expected, but his body was beginning to let him down. Having been very active in the AIDS community, he was well aware of his situation. I helped him out where I could. Among the errands he asked of me one day was to post a letter, together with a coupon, to a company offering a free trip to the Caribbean to a lucky winner in several months time. I remember walking some way to the nearest post box wondering why I was doing this obviously pointless task. But I knew that such dreams were part of what was keeping him alive. In fact, he died two weeks later.

Although I would dearly love to know that my life was 'in order', I have not yet tackled this process. I keep thinking about downsizing, but like St Augustine on the subject of chastity, I say, "Oh Lord, not yet." I have thrown away a lot of papers, given away many books and made some lists that will make life easier for my children when they come to cope with my death. But I have not yet moved from our large family house of forty years, and still own a lot of things that should properly be moved elsewhere.

More importantly, I have numerous projects still to go. I am nearly finished one book and am planning another. There are books I want to read. My family photographs are in a mess and need to be sorted if those who remain behind want to know who was who. A long list of Things To Be Done sits on my desk.

And there are aims for the future that will never get finished. I want to see my grandsons grow up and find out what they choose to do with their lives. If I live long enough, I will feel the same about any potential great-grandchildren. So, there is no end ever in sight.

In truth, we don't stop until we are stopped. At that point, we will be in the middle of loads of things. There will always be a long To Do list. In short, we will be in the middle of a sentence.

And this is how it should be.

STORIES FROM MY LIFE

The Special Needs Unit

1986

Because of the work I used to do, I would sometimes find myself in a very odd place, wondering how in the world I got there. It was one of those occasions. A colleague and I were eating lunch in the cafeteria of an Adult Training Centre, a kind of day centre for people with learning disabilities aged 18 or over, which no longer seems to exist. The food was basic and there were a lot of trainees milling around. The staff were talking to my colleague and me about their Special Needs Unit, which we were due to visit after lunch. One man seemed to be trying to catch my eye, and I assumed that he was one of the trainees. I later learned he was the Director of the Unit. Another lesson learned.

My working life must be seen as a very odd business to most people. I never had jobs with a single focus nor any sense of permanency. I was what is called a social researcher – initially very junior and eventually senior – in the fields of health and social care. Contracts are inevitably short term, whereby three years is a long time and six months is not unknown. Every job must be found or created, either by applying to

assist on someone else's project or by designing and
successfully funding your own. When in the mid 1980s, I went
fully freelance, my working life became even more
unpredictable, as I could get requests to work for a few weeks
or even days. I never knew what I would be doing next,
including the potential to be wholly unemployed. And, like an
actor, it kept me on my toes, as I felt I was seen as only as
good as my last job.

But it was also fascinating. I was a qualitative researcher,
asking people questions and analysing the information
thereby gained. Over time, I carried out a mixture of
individual interviews and focus groups on all sorts of subjects.
I was constantly learning and challenging myself to cope in
fields well outside my general knowledge. I enjoyed this
aspect immensely.

I also gained the opportunity to meet all kinds of people and
to see all kinds of situations. I interviewed unemployed
people, many of whose impoverished circumstances were
saddening indeed. I interviewed numerous middle-to-senior
staff in local councils who were inevitably surprised that
anyone would be interested in their thoughts. Following an
interview with a senior doctor at the Royal College of
Surgeons, I was given a personal tour of the building, with its
own museum – to the great annoyance of his secretary as he
had another appointment. I once even found myself in the
plush spacious office of a very senior civil servant, who asked
me – much to my surprise – how I would spend £1 million for
a particular purpose. And even more to my surprise, some
months later a major programme was announced, including
my suggestions.

But of all these situations, the one I remember most vividly was the visit to the Special Needs Unit that day. The day centre provided activities for those who had finished school and the attendees were all adults living at home with their parents. The Unit was for those at the least capable end of any scale, who needed a great deal of help. Staff at the day centre were very keen that we visit this unit, although it was not actually relevant to our research.

The most memorable part of this visit was the director, so very self-effacing that we did not recognise him when he sought our attention at lunch. This man, whose name I have long forgotten, was one of the most quietly impressive people I have ever had the privilege to meet. He was coping with what many people would consider the most difficult end of humanity and he was giving them dignity. He clearly loved his work and the 15 or so people in his charge and he recounted a number of stories about them.

First, he told us that he had managed to toilet train every single one of them, although none had been capable of looking after themselves in that department when they arrived. It had taken time and patience (as, indeed, any mother would know), but it could be done and he had done it. All the parents, of course, were thrilled, as this simple act greatly eased their lives at home.

Second, he had somehow got most of them to a stage where they could take part in ordinary day-to-day activities, from which they had been shielded all their lives. He told us of taking them on walks and one young man loved to walk on the low walls in front of houses, like children do, but he had never had the chance. His mother was delighted.

And one evening, he took a small group to the local pub. Afterwards, he had to take them all to their individual homes. One man, perhaps in his thirties, had drunk too much. The director told us how nervous he had been when he delivered this slightly inebriated man to his mother and rather expected to be heavily chastised for allowing him to get into this state. Instead, she burst into tears. She said she had thought he would never have the opportunity for such a normal experience – and thanked him profusely.

There was also a young woman in her twenties or so who was entirely inapproachable. She was both blind, deaf and unable to speak and seemed unable to know who or where she was. She sat on the floor in the middle of the room, rocking back and forth. It was heart-breaking to watch her.

My colleague and I were both shaken and highly moved by the whole experience. We had seen something we never expected to see, that few people ever do see. People with any form of learning disability are often very vulnerable, but these were at another level. And certainly much more hidden from the rest of us.

It took a long time for us to regain our sense of balance, of normality.

Beatification

1990

The letter arrived late one Friday afternoon with embossed letterhead. It was from the President of Mount Holyoke College, an excellent American women's college with which I had had no connection whatsoever. It told me that they wished to award me an honorary doctorate and asked me to contact them about arrangements. I was not yet fifty, had been in my view a good social researcher and published frequently, but never anyone of eminence. In our more modern parlance, it seemed an honour above my pay grade.

My first thought was to wonder if it could be a hoax, but I couldn't think of anyone I knew who would want to – and be able to – pull it off. The letterhead seemed genuine enough. I immediately phoned my parents, both of whom had been in the sort of jobs where one might possibly expect an honorary degree, but neither had ever been awarded one. They were absolutely thrilled. My father called it my "beatification" and, I am sure, bored all his friends with the news.

I was more concerned with its veracity. On the Monday, I phoned the office of the President of the College and a secretary answered. On hearing my question, she immediately said, "I don't know anything about this." Well, I thought, perhaps it really is a hoax. But, of course, it turned out that no one had informed her of the letter and it was, indeed, genuine.

They were eager for me to come and receive the degree the following May. I had already booked a trip to the US in April, plus a work trip to Belgium, and did not really fancy another journey across the Atlantic so soon. I might add that I also dislike public ceremonies and had never attended any of my own graduation ceremonies (BA, MA or PhD). I said, somewhat hesitantly, that it would be awkward and wondered whether they could possibly send it to me. Well, in that case, I was told, we will award it another year. At which point, I realised I might as well go now and get it over with. Perhaps it would be fun.

And that was the beginning of the only short week in my life where I felt like Someone Important. It was no small thing, after all, to be awarded an honorary doctorate and, for those brief days, I was treated − and felt − like someone of distinction. My one regret was that I was not being asked to talk to the graduating class. I liked the idea of giving a talk to a set of intelligent young women about being "on the threshold of life."

When the time came, I flew to New York and took the train to Massachusetts. I had to stand most of the way, because it was a holiday weekend and trains were full. I remember thinking to myself "I am getting an honorary degree and ought to be given a seat", but I kept quiet. Who cared?

There were several others getting an honorary degree − a young female playwright who had gone to Mount Holyoke (who gave the speech I had wanted to give), an Afro-American man who was the President of Howard University and said he might arrange a degree for me there (but, sadly, I never heard from him), and a French scientist from a Paris Institute who had made some discovery related to cancer.

74

We were all carefully looked after for the whole weekend. I had been assigned a young economics professor whose job was to make me feel welcome. I remember him driving me to local scenic areas. I did ask why I had been chosen and he said that it was all done by a committee, but the person who nominated me was away and he honestly didn't know. And I never did find out.

The degree ceremony was wonderful and terrible at the same time. We all had the usual honorary robes (one part of which I was allowed to take home and remains in my closet untouched) and after walking on ceremoniously, we sat on the stage. Following the usual speeches, each graduate came up to the college President, who handed over her bachelor's degree, shook her hand, smiled warmly and said something personal. I was sitting very close and was incredibly impressed that she was equally warm and welcoming with the last graduate as she had been with the first.

But it was also very long. I don't like sitting still for a long time. I knew I shouldn't fidget in front of everyone. My mind was wandering all over the place and, at one point, I wondered how long we had to go. It was then that I realised that the girls were being called to the stage in alphabetical order and we were up to G. There were roughly five hundred of them.

At the end, each of us receiving honorary degrees were also invited to stand, were read a letter of commendation and, in turn, shook the President's hand. They had done their homework and my commendation did, indeed, reflect the work I had done. And so passed my beatification.

My parents had come to watch and, after it was all over, they drove me back to their country house about two hours drive away in the Catskill mountains in New York State. And, as a special present, they had arranged for me to fly in a small plane from nearby Albany to JFK airport, an unforgettable trip down the beautiful Hudson River, flying much lower than most airplanes. As a bonus, it also allowed me to miss all the hassle and the traffic of New York City on a holiday weekend.

It had been a heady few days. Yes, I did feel 'Important'. About a day after getting home, my then nine-year-old son brought me back to earth with some comment.

Where I have remained ever since.

Italian National Pride

1991

Some children, I have noted, tend to have a passionate attachment to certain things, which change regularly over time but are very intense while they last. I wasn't like that, but my sister was. My daughter wasn't, but my son was. The particular passions were always unpredictable and their genesis was not always clear, but while they lasted, you knew well what interested them. For my son, one year, it was understanding the planets and the stars; another, it was memorising all the countries of the world, complete with their capitals and their flags.

Around the age of eight, he developed a passion for semi-precious stones. He liked to collect them and he liked to wear them on the odd occasion. He went through my paltry jewellery box and took out a few items that interested him. Indeed, I have a picture of him wearing about six necklaces and bracelets on both wrists, all worn over blue jean shorts and a striped football shirt. Nothing remotely girly. Of course, we picked up interesting stones for him from beaches from time to time and even bought him the occasional gemstone, such as an amethyst.

In 1991, when he was ten, we had gone to the Amalfi coast, with various side trips including one to Herculaneum. It was a lovely day and an interesting site. A shop was selling boxes with collections of different gemstones, which he wanted to buy with his own money. My memory was that it cost about £10 (in Lira), which was a sizeable sum in those days for a young boy, to be taken from his pocket money. But he chose to do so and was very proud of his purchase.

After a long visit to the site, we went off to find some lunch. When that was over and we were wandering around the area, we realised we no longer had the package with the stones. The reasonable assumption was that we had accidentally left the package in the restaurant. Of course, we went back to find them, but were told by the manager that no package had been found. He even checked with someone else there, but it was clear that they were not there.

We spent some time retracing our steps, looking everywhere for the package with little hope and, indeed, no luck. We were all feeling very low and my son was, not surprisingly close to tears. Because we needed to take a train and we were far from the station, we found a taxi to take us back in good time. The taxi driver saw immediately that something was wrong. His English was minimal and my Italian only slightly better, but somehow he communicated his concern and wanted to know the problem. When I explained the situation, he asked for the details of our restaurant and drove us there. We waited outside, with little hope, but he returned after a few minutes with our package.

My son, of course, was thrilled to see his purchase again. But the taxi driver was very upset and, indeed, angry. Whether he knew our particular restaurant I do not know, but he clearly knew that tourist spots like it were happy to keep any parcels left by accident and, presumably, re-sell their contents. I never understood everything he said, but he communicated that he was highly ashamed of any such practice and the reputation it gave to his country. In recompense, he refused to allow us to pay any fare. Italian honour had been saved.

And my son still has the stones.

Chapter 3: BUT MUCH REMAINS THE SAME: THE GOOD PARTS

Introduction

One of the key aspects of being old is hidden in plain sight. Nobody talks about it. Perhaps nobody thinks about it. But it is the simple fact that the lives of most older people are generally full of all the things they did before. Of course, they may drop some activities from choice or changed circumstances and, perhaps for the same reasons, they will gain others. But for many of us, we continue to live along much the same lines as we lived ten, twenty, or even thirty or more years before.

This is really not so surprising. Through trial and error, we find the things we like to do in life and we keep doing them. This chapter explores some of the things I like to do and therefore have done for years. It is necessarily only a small proportion of the many activities I could have written about. I have left out the joys of settling down with a good book or going to a powerful movie or listening to moving music. Or cooking well-loved meals. There is little about travel or pottering in the garden. You can't tell all of life.

These may not be the things that you most like to do. Indeed, you may not like doing them at all. But I write about them here as a chance to ponder on the broad issue of the things we do as we pass through life. They range from pastimes that heighten the senses and therefore bring a kind of spirituality into life — singing, doing yoga, volunteering — to the very mundane — having a chat and a lie-down. Taken altogether, they are the meat and drink of everyday life.

Now and before.

Singing

I was only age seven or eight and my class was singing. A teacher was playing the piano and the combination of the group singing, together with the accompaniment, gave me a moment of those strange goosebumps that music can suddenly bring on. It was a new and very powerful sensation and, perhaps as a result, I still remember the song — "Welcome, sweet springtime, we greet thee with song." Thanks to the then never-imagined internet, I now know that this is an old song, composed in the late nineteenth century. I would probably find it much too saccharine now, but it was my introduction to the palpable power of music.

Indeed, it was evidently not my first introduction to music per se. Most of us were expected to sing as children — whether at school or in church or within the family — and I was no exception. My mother used to sit down at the piano and play songs for my brother and me to sing with her. I quite enjoyed those sessions and learned a lot of songs, particularly from a book of old English folk songs. Not all of them were suited for children. I never could understand the rather melancholic lament of a woman who "used to wear my apron low" but now wore it "high." Indeed, I am told that I caused a stir in my nursery school, when my very proper teacher asked what we would like to sing. "What shall we do with the drunken sailor?" I proposed. I thought it was a rousing good tune. She did not approve.

As an older child, I sang in the school choir and found that a very joyous and satisfying activity. I sang the alto part and loved the challenge of not singing the tune, but thereby making the whole sound better. I still do. I once sang a duet in the school assembly from Benjamin Britten's Ceremony of Carols, which was very frightening at the time but pleasing to have done.

And then came a long lull. I never joined a choir at university, nor anywhere else, because I thought I would not be good enough. The longer that went on, the stronger that feeling became. Then, in my early 50s, I was invited, along with all parents, to sing in the parents' choir of my son's school. I dithered for some time about whether to try to join, but finally concluded that if I were auditioned and turned down, I could live with myself. There was no audition.

And for well over twenty-five years, I have sung in that choir, followed by one other. We generally sing serious music, like Brahms' Requiem or a Mozart Mass or even Bach, but we do branch out to other things from time to time. We even sang

Bohemian Rhapsody by Queen. It was one of Queen Elizabeth's Jubilees and our choir conductor, who had a great sense of fun, proposed this to mark the occasion instead of the usual renditions of regal songs.

Choirs have seen a real resurgence in recent years and I am not surprised. Singing with others somehow creates a real bond between you because the whole is so much better than the sum of the parts. You struggle with the hard parts together and triumph together when you get it right. It can be frustrating when things go wrong, but oh so wonderful when everyone is singing well. And, of course, there is the pleasure of performance – to sing beautiful music for the benefit of others is a wonderful activity, whether in a church or concert hall.

And the cherry on top is that singing anywhere – choir, bath or wherever – is very good for your health, so they tell me. It is good for the lungs and good overall exercise. Certainly, when I am feeling low, I always feel much better after a good sing.

I will continue to sing with my choir as long as it is possible. Even during lockdown, I carried on with a rather pallid sing-along on Zoom, which was only just a little better than doing nothing at all. And singing is something you can do at any age. The members of my choir range from their early twenties to one woman in her mid-nineties.

I don't know everyone by name, but I know we have a bond in common.

"My granny likes to stand on her head"

When my older grandson, now in his teens, was a toddler, he loved to watch me stand on my head, which I had learned in yoga. He tried to copy me with little success, but I discouraged him in any case, as I was told that standing on your head is not good for a small child. My daughter subsequently told me that he went into his nursery school and said to his teacher, "My granny likes to stand on her head." I never heard what her response was, but I liked the sentence.

And he was right. I did – and despite being in my late-70s, I still do. It's all down to yoga.

Unless they have been doing yoga for years, most older people probably wouldn't think of trying it. They see their daughters doing it, but think they are too old. Perhaps they feel it requires you to look like the young and supple women in most yoga pictures. But it doesn't. People of all shapes, sizes and ages can do yoga. It is not a matter of putting on a leotard and aiming to look beautiful. My class is full of grandmothers like me. And we are all devoted to it, rain or shine. It makes us feel better.

I was slow to discover yoga for myself. I wish I had done so earlier. Years ago, when I thought I should be doing more exercise to keep fit, several friends suggested I try yoga. When I asked what happened there, I was told you went into odd poses and held them for a while. This seemed a rather bizarre thing to do – and certainly appeared to have little to do with exercise. I was not drawn to the idea and did not pursue it.

But how wrong I was. In the end, I started yoga in my early fifties because I had back problems. I had gone to a very good osteopath, whose ministrations would work for a while, but then wear off after a week or two. She encouraged me to try yoga to get my body stronger, so that any changes she produced might last longer. That sounded sensible and I overcame my initial prejudice. The result was that I got much stronger. And I didn't need the osteopath anymore. And I loved yoga.

Some yoga involves a lot of movement and feels very much like an exercise class. The type I eventually went for – Iyengar yoga – is slow and purposeful, but my goodness, you do get your muscles, both internal and external, exercised. The strange postures are there for that purpose. I realised I needed to separate being visibly active from being equally – but less visibly – so. Yoga works our system all over.

The result is both subtle and profound. I slowly began to feel more supple – or "bendy" as one friend put it. All sorts of day-to-day movements became easier, which is both pleasing and practical, especially as we age. My balance was definitely better. It is hard to judge, but they say breathing becomes easier. My health, which was always good, certainly remained so.

And yoga is more than exercise. It puts you in touch with your own body, making you feel more in tune with its ways. One friend, a yoga teacher, said that it "wakes your body up and gives it a good shake." It helps us to rediscover the joys of actively using our body, rather than seeing it as something we carry around without much thought. I also find that it requires so much concentration that I forget the things that are worrying me and feel much more refreshed as a result. Some people find that they even like themselves more.

Lockdown proved a real problem for those of us who take their yoga seriously. Enthusiastic as I am, I found it hard to do it on my own at home. It is so much easier to take the 'orders' of the teacher, as well as to have the reassurance that she is watching to ensure I do a posture properly. Indeed, I have always said that the brilliance of my particular teacher was knowing when we should be discouraged from a particular posture because it would be bad for our individual body such as a bad back, but also knowing when we should be pushed because our reluctance is simple laziness.

When one teacher decided to set up Zoom classes, I went back with pleasure.

Writing

I was eight years old. It was an ordinary Saturday, but my father – rather unusually – needed to go to work for some urgent matter. They probably didn't know what to do with me –perhaps my mother was away on work, she was from time to time – so he took me to his office. I was given some paper and pens and was told to sit quietly at a big table. The idea came to me to write the story of my life (I would not have known the word 'autobiography'). I had one line for each age, ending with the memorable statement "age 8: And then I understood what life was." For some reason, I didn't know why at the time, my parents thought this was very funny. They kept this document safe and I found it with their papers – and the jacks I used to play with at more or less the same time – after they had died.

Did this show that I was to become a writer for much of my life? Who knows. No, I did not produce a novel at the age of twelve. But for as long as I can remember, I just liked the process of writing. I enjoyed the challenge of working out how to begin, how to find the right word for the context and, perhaps most importantly, how to prune my thoughts when appropriate. The rhythm of a sentence is important to me, whether reading it or writing it. I never read anything I have written without tweaking it in some way. Indeed, I love the process of editing, which I compare to pruning weeds – just as a garden can suddenly have a shape and a beauty when the weeds have gone, so too can a piece of writing.

One might think I would have aimed to be a writer from the start – a novelist, say. But I felt that such an occupation required much more experience of life. And it was not seen as a 'real' career, which I wanted early on. Most importantly, it would not support my husband through his PhD. I turned to other pursuits.

For years, I didn't identify as a writer as such, although I did a lot of writing as part of my day-to-day work as a social researcher. I wrote numerous reports, articles and, yes, even books on the topics of my research. I liked doing this, others seemed to like what I produced and so it went on year after year. Fairly early on, I chose to work freelance, which meant I undertook whatever service was wanted from me. (I used to say, "Like the oldest profession in the world, I sell my time.") I was asked to do a lot of writing – research proposals, reports from Committees of Inquiry or for Government departments – as well as editing.

At one point, someone I had never met asked me what I did for a living and I said I was a writer. That felt strange, but correct. Even after retirement, I carried on doing unpaid what I had previously done for pay, because it was what I liked to do.

I was, of course, paid for my writing when it was commissioned, but once – just once – my writing skills brought benefits of no compare. I had been working at my desk when an email arrived, inviting me to win a luxury weekend in Paris for two. All I needed to do was to write why I liked Eurostar Frequent Traveller (rather like Air Miles) in 25 words or less. I was captured and spent the next ten minutes writing a little ditty, despite the fact that there was no poetry whatsoever in the name. Yet I discovered a Big problem – it was 29 words and sometimes people took these details seriously. I spent another ten or more minutes trying to cut it down, decided my attempt was not worth the candle and also decided I needed to get back to work. With no enthusiasm, I sent in my feeble 25 words and forgot all about it.

Yet a month later, a second email arrived with the news that I had won. It took me a minute to remember what it was, as I had completely forgotten the exercise. But I really had won. In the fullness of time, I received two first class return tickets to Paris, a voucher for two nights for two in the Hotel Crillon (the last time I had been nearby, there was a crowd of teenagers because Michael Jackson was staying there), a voucher for a meal for two at Le Cinq (three Michelin stars, as high as you can get) in the Hotel Georges Cinq – and a voucher for two helicopter tickets for an hour's trip over Paris. Plus some other vouchers to ensure we weren't out of pocket on other meals. All in all, when we added up the estimated value, it came to something like £2500. I have never ever, before or since, been paid £100 per word.

People do occasionally ask whether I would recommend writing as an activity to take on in old age. My response is why not – If someone has the inclination, feels they 'have a book in them' and want to try. Some may find a whole new career, writing down stories they told their children or difficult experiences from their lives. But if anyone is after fame or, indeed, an easy income, it is definitely not a good idea. It is possible to become rich and famous as a writer, but it is exceedingly unlikely. But it is a great way to challenge oneself and do something that is genuinely creative.

The day I decide to stop will be a sad day.

Having a lie-down

It happens quite often these days. My husband wants to mull over some issue or impart some news and, instead of doing so there and then, he says, "Let's have a lie-down, so we can talk." We go into the bedroom, take off our shoes, lie down and start to chat. It can last five minutes or twenty or sometimes more. We can move onto other topics. But it is relaxing, intimate and very easy to talk. Indeed, it is incredibly restorative.

Usually, any discussions of the joys of bed refer to one of two things: the pleasures of a good night's sleep or, alternatively, sex. I am a great believer in both, but they are not the issue here. Instead, lying down together is a wonderful way to give each other time to discuss anything at all. It is a time to review ideas, mull over plans for the future or just explore how you are feeling about life in general. Although it may result in some broad or even particular decisions, I don't think it should feel too purposeful. On the contrary, it is time to let your mind wander over anything, including your relationship.

Of course, I also lie down on my own, simply to renew my energy and get a rest. This could happen when I was younger, but it is needed much more often as I age. I find a number of friends also say the same, especially the older ones. Some of us begin to take a nap – either every day or now and then. I am reluctant to take a proper (sleeping) nap, because it leaves me unable to get to sleep at night. I envy those who can do so with impunity. But there is nonetheless a great benefit in a rest. I can listen to the radio or to audio books (I favour programmes stored on my iPod for this purpose). Or just lie there and think my own thoughts. It is a very peaceful thing to do.

In contrast, lying down with someone else is clearly a very intimate activity, even when nothing physical is involved.

Being prone on a bed seems to make you let down your guard, so that you are more willing to talk easily. Sometimes, the fact that you can't actually see each other makes it less intimidating than sitting at a table or in a living room. It is not surprising that it is the chosen posture for people in some forms of psychotherapy.

Interestingly, lying down together can also be a time of intimacy with other family members. One grandson, who spends roughly one night a week at our house, loves to climb into bed with his grandfather in the morning. Long ago, said grandfather had agreed to sleep in the nearby spare room to allay any worries in the night. This early morning time has become one of many rituals, when they talk about anything and everything, and is sadly missed if for any reason (like waking up too late to have the time before school) it is impossible.

An Indian woman in my book about grandmothers also describes such moments with her grandchildren as very special, the combination of touching them and talking with them:

"You can't buy that happiness anywhere," she says.

Eating out

It used to be so simple. We would suddenly decide, "let's go out for lunch" and there was one place to which we would inevitably head. Yes, it required a short tube ride, but it was such a pleasure when we got there. The premises were not fancy, but the food was beautifully cooked tapas of all kinds, brought to the table hot from the kitchen. Because we ate there frequently, we got to know the people who ran it and could joke with them about all sorts of things. And then, about two years ago, they told us the sad news that they were closing. We never managed to replace it. And then lockdown changed everything for everyone.

For all my adult life, I have loved to eat out. Despite the fact that I am a moderately good cook, there is so much to be said for it. First, it is such a nice way to make an 'occasion'. We put on somewhat nicer clothes – and, for some restaurants, *much* nicer clothes – and feel we are already in a different-from-normal situation. We are waited on, of course, and have the pleasure of choosing what we feel like. We can sit and talk for as long as we want, with someone bringing food or drink as needed. If it is somewhere with a view, so much the better.

And it also gives the chance to eat food we don't normally eat – and even sometimes discover something I could make at home. If I am keen on a dish, I will ask the chef how he makes it. I also love the way some restaurants make food look especially inviting. We do that a little at home, but with much less of the flair – no swirls in the soup or parsley artfully scattered.

Sometimes, it is simply a matter of presenting food in a particular order. We once had an anniversary dinner at a plush hotel, with a handsome room with wood panelling. At the end of the meal, after a very delicious dessert, the waiter brought a large basket of big dark cherries – just the thing to settle the digestion after a large meal. Every time I eat cherries, I think of that occasion.

I have some clear memories of particular meals, often served outdoors somewhere on the continent. A very unpretentious hotel in the Basque area of Spain, when asked if they could rustle up something simple in the evening (because we didn't want to drive elsewhere) produced a dish of prawns and herbed vegetables and I can't remember what else, beautifully laid out. The restaurant in the Auvergne with a seven-course vegetarian meal; the place had lost its Michelin star, but we had an old Michelin Guide and did not know that.

The seafood platter served on the terrace of a hotel in the Alps, not far from Chamonix, which was not only delicious but was accompanied by a far-off dramatic small avalanche within our view. I could go on.

But there are some things I don't like at all about eating out. I don't like the bowing and scraping of waiters in elegant restaurants, asking constantly, "Did you enjoy the meal?" I don't want my napkin put into my lap when I sit down. I don't want a waiter pouring my wine or water every time I take a few sips. Indeed, one of our tests of a good restaurant is whether the waiter will desist from this, once we make it clear we prefer to pour our drinks ourselves.

Eating out should feel like there is a mutual pleasure between provider and provided-for. You may or may not meet the chef, but the person bringing the food should feel enthusiastic about it and greet your enthusiasm with warmth, not formality. Preferably, they make you feel that they want nothing better than to please you. Such restaurants are hard to find, but they are the ones we keep going back to.

But since Covid-19 has been upon us, we have not eaten out once. For some of the time, restaurants were closed, but even when they were open, there was a sense of danger in being around other people. I didn't fancy being served by people in masks. It changes the nature of the occasion.

One of life's pleasures to look forward to.

Chatting

It is late morning and the phone rings. I look at the phone – young people won't know that you never used to know who was calling until they told you or you recognised their voice – and think, oh great, it's my daughter, we can have a nice chat. We talk frequently and it is a good way to relax, but also to keep in touch. She will tell me about how her work is going or what her son is up to or what she is doing for the weekend. Rarely anything hugely important, although that can happen, but a pleasing way to pass the time in the company of someone you love. And keep abreast of the day-to-day fabric of their lives.

I have always liked to chat. With my husband, I chat first thing in the morning about any problems in the night, I chat at lunch about events of the morning and I chat in the evening about the rest of the day. There is always something to chat about – some small disturbance in the local supermarket, family news from our children, problems with the computer, the characters in the book I am reading, a programme seen on TV. The list goes on and on.

Of course, I also chat to friends and neighbours. The status of the latter in our lives is interesting because they are on the borderline of people you know well and those you don't know at all. I have got to know a number of neighbours over time simply through the medium of casual chat, as we meet by chance. We can now have lengthy discussions about the state of the world or the schooling of our grandchildren. Such talks can be so engrossing that my husband begins to worry what happened to me when I had only popped out for some milk. In small ways, they enrich the day.

Chatting seems so inconsequential, one might well ask how anyone could even think of writing about it. Yet stop to think about how important it is. Whether undertaken with a spouse, other family members or friends and neighbours, chatting is the glue that holds people together. Talking about everyday mundane matters is the way we come to feel part of one another. Strangely enough, it is probably one of the more intimate things we do, aside from the obvious.

And chatting can take place anywhere. On the phone or in person. You can chat online with such vehicles as Zoom or Skype, but it's not very satisfactory. It may be at the dinner table, lying on a sofa or – especially – in bed. Those early morning chats, before even getting up, are a lovely way to start the day.

Chatting is not the same as small talk, the meaningless discussions you have at parties with people you've never met before and probably won't meet again. Especially after the lack of engagement created by small talk. The British can talk endlessly about the weather. Not me. My absolute bête noire is how we got here – "Oh, you took the M11 to Cambridge? I know it's the shortest, but it can get so congested before you get onto it and I hate sitting in traffic, so I took the A1 which is easy...." And I am asleep. Or worse, just bored.

Spending such apparently trivial time with close friends and family allows us to keep up with their lives – what they are thinking about, excited about or, indeed, worrying about. And telling them about ourselves. And it can also lead to other things. Even a brief moment talking to a neighbour over the proverbial garden fence can lead to a cup of tea, the discovery of shared interests and, eventually, the possibility of helping each other in some way or, indeed, becoming close friends.

Of course, we have much more significant discussions with people we are close to. You can call such discussions chat or not. I probably wouldn't, on their own. But, in fact, in the course of such conversations, we move quickly from issues which are important to ones that are less important and back again. That is part of the pleasure of such activity.

In some circles, the concept of chatting is looked down on as suitably preceded by the word 'mindless'. It is seen as synonymous with 'gossip', 'chatter', 'jabber', 'babble' or the like. And we certainly all know people who tend to go on and on until we want to scream. But it is quite wrong, in my view, to conflate the concepts of chatting and babbling. The former is, above all, creating a sense of connectedness to other people. And the opposite of chatting is having no one to talk to or, in a word, loneliness. A recently widowed friend told me that what she missed was the day-to-day chat about matters of no great significance.

For years, loneliness was seen as something to be ashamed of and few people were willing to admit to it. It is now slowly coming out of the closet as an issue to be taken seriously, with growing media attention and efforts to overcome it. Long may they thrive.

Much better to chat with someone.

Volunteering

It was a beautiful spring day. Sun was streaming in from the window of the hospice. A young man with AIDS had asked if I would mind sitting with him for a moment. He loved opera and had a CD player in his room. He put on the famous duet from the Pearl Fishers and we sat, each in our own thoughts, listening to the aria. It was one of those special occasions that arose only at the moment.

I had been volunteering at this hospice for several years and I loved the unexpected moments that it brought. Yet the first time I ever walked into a hospice, I did so with some trepidation, concerned about what horrible things I was about to encounter. I was completely taken aback that all I found was an incredible sense of tranquillity. It drew me in, I wanted to be part of the place. So much so that I applied soon after to a local hospice, was interviewed briefly and that was it. No background check, no training, just thrown in at the deep end. That was nearly thirty years ago. It would be different now.

I spent roughly four hours in the hospice every Saturday afternoon. It had only 16 beds and was almost always full. People were admitted much earlier than they would be now. All were dying, but some lived for months. My job was to talk to patients, especially those with no visitors, make them tea and discuss the menu for the next day. It felt daunting when I started, but I quickly became adept at making appropriate small conversation. Visits generally went smoothly.

But now and again, I would be faced with something difficult, often funny at the time. One week, around the time of Mad Cow Disease, there was beef on the menu. People In England had become uneasy about eating beef, although it was said to take twenty years for infected meat to have an impact. But yes, one patient studied the menu and asked, "do you think I dare to eat the beef?" I said I thought it would be ok, trying not to smile. As I don't have a natural poker face, this was not easy.

More difficult was a father who had travelled from the South of France to see his son, who was dying of AIDS. He clearly had not known his son was gay nor that he was ill, so it was a lot for him to take in. I felt hugely sorry for him, so far from home, with no English. I had mentioned to a nurse that I spoke some French, but did not expect to be confronted with a thick Provencal accent, famously difficult to decipher. He began to pour out his heart. I understood exactly what was going on, but it was a strain to get the particulars. I decided to answer when I could, but otherwise, to repeat, with as sympathetic air as I could muster, shaking my head from side to side, *"c'est tres difficile"* ("it's very difficult.") I have never forgotten that man's pain. Nor my struggle.

I worked at the hospice for four years. I loved the feeling that in some not-easily-defined way, I was helping people at this important time in their lives. I had to stop because my husband and I had decided to travel a lot and I could no longer guarantee to be there every week. I found the experience so interesting that, much later, I wrote a book based on interviews with hospice nurses, doctors and many others talking about the joys and challenges of such work and its impact on their lives.

For me, it felt important just to be there at this very intimate time.

Looking into our ancestors

When my son was a small child (five or six), he heard about the concept of infinity and, like many children, was fascinated by it. He also began to realise that there were generations within families, with some coming before, like his grandparents, and some after. He was late to this particular concept because we had so few relatives who he ever saw.

One morning, he put the two thoughts together. "You know, Mum," he said, "the people coming before us were not infinity, but the people coming after us are infinity." His English wasn't up to the task of expressing his thought, but the thought itself was profound, indeed.

There is something about finding ourselves in our sixties or older that makes our heads turn to the past in general and to our ancestry in particular. I have no idea why this comes so forcefully at this time. Perhaps as we age, our sense of time means that the decades before we were born seem less long ago and our ancestors therefore seem more real and present. In any case, there seem to be an awful lot of them, despite them not being infinite.

Some people take genealogy very seriously, signing up to all sorts of websites and checking through censuses well into the past. This seems like a great pastime, which can keep people busy for years. But some of us learn about our ancestry by somewhat more accidental – or, indeed, lazy – means. We may benefit from the hard work of someone else in the family. I discovered in recent years that a surprising number of my forebears were keen on memoir-writing, so documents have turned up within the family from different periods and even in different languages. To add to the fun, these are not always consistent in their description of the same events. The truth, as any historian would confirm, is hard to know. But it is fun to try.

I occasionally wonder what people are hoping to discover. Someone famous? A connection to royalty? A murderer? My parents were highly respectable, so my ancestors might be expected to be respectable, too. And many of them were. The problem is that these are invariably the least interesting to read about. They had a respectable job, had a certain number of children and died. But fortunately, I have come up with some relatives with more doubtful qualities. One fairly distant ancestor was an explorer in the South Seas in the late nineteenth century, evidently selling tobacco on the side. When he came on one group of islanders who didn't know what to do with this product, he set up smoking classes, thereby securing a demand for his regular return. I shouldn't be proud of this man, but I have to admit that I admire his ingenuity. And he wasn't to know about the link with cancer, after all.

A much closer relative (my great-grandfather) was involved as a young man in import-export dealings on the Mexican-US border around the turn of the 20th century. This was not genteel territory and it would appear that there were some measured judgments about the declaration of silver at the border. As the proceeds of import taxes were said to end up in the pockets of those collecting them, the moral issue could be said to be unclear. In any case, he ended up a very rich man. And, as history often shows, the money was completely lost by his son, my grandfather, in a series of ill-judged enterprises. He ended up as a door-to-door salesman in the 1920s and '30s, with a sense of permanent shame.

Once we have looked into our forebears, we have to wonder what to do with the information. Does it help us to understand ourselves better? I am not so sure. But I did end up feeling more clearly like one link in an inexorable chain.

Climate change or other disasters notwithstanding, an infinite one.

When do people stop having sex?

People everywhere are fascinated by sex. I am not the first to say so. We wonder what other people do and when and what it means to them. And some wonder how long it continues. Of all the stories I tell about my family, the one which always gains immediate attention is this one about my father.

My parents lived in an independent apartment in a retirement community in Pennsylvania. They moved in when they were both about 80 and died ten years later, within three months of each other, roughly twenty years ago. After about five years, my mother developed vascular dementia. This is, of course, every married person's worst fear. The husband or wife is no longer what they once were, but you are still married. And it is harder and harder to cope with the sheer physical demands.

My mother remained in the family apartment for well over a year, with a carer hired to help with her daily needs. But eventually, it was too much for my father to manage and it was agreed that she would move to the Assisted Living section of the community. She was looked after and he could pop in several times a day to see her. He rarely complained, at least to me. It was just something that had happened.

In the meantime, his eyesight had become much worse and he was losing one of his great pleasures – reading. He listened to a lot of audiobooks (and complained that there was no easy way to find the place where you fell asleep). He had a friend, a somewhat younger woman, who came in to read to him. He was terribly pleased about this and talked about it – and her – quite frequently in our regular phone calls.

I should have seen it coming. When a man starts mentioning a woman (or vice versa) quite often, it tends to mean that something more than friendship is involved. But it just didn't occur to me. My very perceptive daughter suggested that it was a possibility and I thought, no, that is unlikely. Not because the thought upset me, but they just seemed too old.

I went to visit around the time of his 90th birthday, when we were holding a party for him. Soon after I arrived, he sat down and clearly wanted to communicate something to me. He had never sought very intimate discussions, but this time was different. He mentioned the name of the woman, who I had not yet met, and said he wanted me to know that they had become 'an item'. I remember thinking the word was odd.

He was very clear. He wanted me to know that this was "not simply kissing and cuddling," it was the real thing. Indeed, he said his doctor thought it was terrific for his health. There was no mention of love, but that did not seem important. The key thing was that he was happy. And he was. He was then 90 and she was 83.

I was surprised, but delighted. Whatever my views about fidelity in marriage, they do not extend to the time when one partner is effectively no longer there. I made this very clear and could see him visibly relax. He had wanted me to know, but had been frightened of my reaction. He said his worst fear was that some other resident would tell my mother, but it did not look like that had happened. He still continued to visit her as before.

They never moved in together, although perhaps they stayed in each other's apartments when I was not there. I did not press for such details. The woman continued to be a regular presence in his life until he died. Indeed, the night he died, she went to the hospital and sat with his body for a long time.

When I was in my twenties, I naively thought that sex was only for the young. It simply did not occur to me that people over forty continued with such activities. This was nothing to do with any connection to childbearing, but simply to the assumption that only the young had an appetite for – or interest in – sexual relationships. As we age, we learn more – about this as well as everything else. There is, of course, much more research now. Surveys will tell you about the extent of sexual activity at different ages. But few of these involve people over 70. And we are often reluctant to raise the issue with people we know.

So, when do people stop having sex? I really don't know. I suspect there is a lot of it about. Certainly, in the retirement community, it was common for couples to spring up quite quickly after the death of a partner. But I do know about my father. And when I tell this story, I have never heard a reaction other than "what a wonderful story" or "so, there's hope then."

And I am sure he would be delighted for the world to know.

STORIES FROM MY LIFE

An unexpected friendship

1991

A lot of people, I find, have a close friend who does not make sense. Someone who just doesn't 'fit' with other aspects of their life and no one from outside can quite understand why they are friends at all. Such friendships can be especially meaningful and sometimes surprising. Often, these are started at school, where the personalities of those involved were unformed and their subsequent life trajectories very different.

My friend of this type was a young man with not long to live. I met him through work when I was close to 50 and he was just under 30. He was German, I was American, both living in London, although we first met at a conference in Belgium. More significantly, he was a gay man and I was a married woman with two children. He had grown up poor in a mining town in Germany and had taken up nursing when he left school at 16 because the only real alternative was becoming a miner. I came from a professional family in New York City and had three degrees.

And he had been living with AIDS for five years, whereas I knew nothing about the disease. He was, indeed, highly active in the HIV/AIDS community, seen as something of a leader amongst them. I liked to keep to myself and never led anybody anywhere.

What did we see in each other? I saw a very bright, sensitive but troubled man, who liked to reflect on deeper issues. I guess he saw some of the same qualities in me, although I never asked him. Our temperaments were in some ways similar. He also liked to challenge himself and those around him – and I found that a very inspiring (and somehow intimate) quality. I also learned that his mother had died when he was eighteen months old and he claimed he had been looking for her (in some unspecified way) all his life. He was friends with a number of older women, of whom I was one. None of us knew each other.

We used to meet fairly often, mostly for lunch, although he did come to my house on several occasions. At one lunch, we first planned what was to become a joint book based on interviews with people with AIDS and HIV, taking place at an international conference he was organising. As is the case with Covid-19 today, the world was awash with statistics regarding the numbers diagnosed, but I was unaware of many personal stories. I knew that these can have a bigger impact on people than statistics. This strengthened our friendship and proved an important milestone for me in creating books based around interviews.

But I want to write about our more poignant lunch. Towards the end of his life, he was in and out of hospital with various ailments and I would visit him there. On one occasion, he said, I thought jokingly, "Let's have lunch next week." I said, "Sure," with a smile. But he meant it. And told me so.

The following week, I turned up at the hospital, finding him very frail and attached to a drip, but in his street clothes. It did not seem remotely feasible to take him outside, but he said he had cleared the venture with the staff. We chatted for a bit and then, being a trained nurse, he unplugged himself from the drip and said, grinning, "Let's go."

It was a beautiful October day, sunny and crisp. There was a good restaurant nearby and we headed toward it very slowly. He was incredibly exuberant about the beauty of the day, conveying to me that feeling for ordinary life that can only come to someone long confined to a hospital bed. Some people stared – he was covered in Kaposi's Sarcoma lesions – but he carried on with dignity.

We ordered lunch and talked about all sorts of things of no great importance. I remember him exclaiming at the presentation of the food – and eating much of it, although his hunger was necessarily limited. I simply marvelled that we were there at all. And when we had finished, we walked slowly, and somewhat sadly, back to the hospital, where he climbed onto his bed and re-attached his drip.

He died about two months later. I sat with him for a long time on the day he died, although I went home and was replaced by another female friend by the time he died. A few months later, yet another older female friend and I scattered his ashes in the sea outside of Brighton, as had been his wish.

We watched the carnations she had bought float slowly away, went for a brief tea and headed home full of unspoken thoughts.

I will never forget either day.

Tits

1997

These days, it is increasingly necessary to give a 'trigger warning' for unsuspecting but vulnerable readers. So here it is, perhaps topsy turvy or back to front. I must warn those readers pruriently hoping to find a little excitement as a result of my title that the tits in question are not my own. Nor those of any friend of mine. They are part of a Picasso painting.

My husband and I have visited the Picasso museum in Paris on a number of occasions over the years. This time was in the late 1990s on one of those cold but beautiful March days when spring is just on the horizon.

We were quietly going around the building, when we noticed a sizeable group of Americans of a certain age, mostly women, having the paintings explained by a young Frenchman. They were well-dressed and very earnest, as Americans tend to be. The guide was clearly interesting and enthusiastic, but his English was somewhat limited. I began to listen in, as one does, primarily in the hopes of learning something about the paintings, although there is inevitably a certain general curiosity as well. At one point, I heard the guide hesitate, pointing to what were clearly oddly-located female breasts on a painting, saying, "What do you call these – shall I say *teets*?"

I looked around at the rather po-faced gathering, wondering whether they – like me – were suppressing a wish to smile, but could see little sign of it. They stared at the painting, taking in his words with due seriousness. The guide carried on with his talk and we moved to another room.

That might have been the end of the story, but I have an irrepressible wish to be helpful whenever the occasion arises. And it may never have arisen except that once we had finished in the gallery, and were enjoying the sun in the courtyard, I noticed the guide having a quiet smoke nearby. I wondered whether to say anything, but the helpful me could not resist.

"*Pardon,*" I said politely, and explained in my middling French that I couldn't help overhearing his difficulty when confronted with a picture of a woman's breasts. He might want to know that a more formal word was 'breast' and that 'tit' had other overtones. He was not embarrassed at all, clearly understood what I was trying to say, and thanked me for my help. Indeed, he seemed genuinely eager to learn, if for no other reason than to keep his job as a guide at the gallery.

But it did not end there. One of the group he had been shepherding saw me talking to him and came up to intervene. She immediately admonished me for saying anything, pointing out that I had not paid for his services and therefore had no right to make any form of correction to his English. The guide and I stood there quietly like guilty children, albeit with a small smile. She walked away, her own pride satisfied.

But it is hard to see Picasso paintings without the echo in my head – teets.

Long distance call to the ICU

2000

My father always enjoyed very good health. He used to say that he had been physically sick only four times in his life – once when each of his three children had been born (a kind of sympathetic labour-by-proxy) and the fourth when Eisenhower won the election in 1952. Certainly, I can never remember him ill in bed at any time.

When he was an old man, we had become very close, even though he lived in Pennsylvania and I lived in London. We talked by phone most days. The only major health crisis had happened in his mid-80s. His kidneys had stopped working and it looked like he would need regular dialysis. He had a great fear of being incapacitated and was threatening to refuse the treatment. For the first time ever, my mother phoned asking me to come as she thought I might convince him to accept the treatment. It felt like a big responsibility, but it also felt kind-of good that I alone might accomplish this.

It was a memorable trip, as I was in fact on holiday in Istanbul when she phoned. Within two days, I had been transported from the centre of that ancient city to my own home in London and then to a high-tech hospital environment in the US. But by the time I arrived, my father's kidneys had begun to function again and the crisis was over. He had already agreed to having a stent fitted in his arm for the dialysis. My trip turned out to be unnecessary and I spent my time chatting and listening to him complain frequently about the stent.

But by the year 2000, he was 90 years old. I knew he would not live forever and could see his energy winding down. Very occasionally, he would talk about dying, with a particular concern about what would happen if he died before my mother, who had vascular dementia. I had been visiting every six months or so and had a visit planned for early October.

That September, he was diagnosed with bladder cancer and was due to undergo chemotherapy. He told me he really didn't want such treatment at his age (who could blame him?) but had agreed reluctantly to the plan. In the event, it was postponed due to a chest infection and his doctors then became sufficiently concerned that he was moved into the local hospital. My brother phoned me to say that it was unclear what was likely to happen, but it didn't look good.

I decided I needed to visit immediately, just in case this was the end, but also decided – I can't now remember why – to phone the hospital to let him know I was coming. I got through to a young doctor who told me that my father was in the Intensive Care Unit. I asked whether it would be possible to speak to him. The very sympathetic doctor said well, there was no telephone in the room where he was, but he would set one up for me.

And so I had what turned out to be our very last conversation, although I did not know this at the time, via phone to his ICU bed. My father said he didn't know what was happening, but if I wanted to see him alive, I should come quickly. I said I would. We chatted briefly about this and that. I remember he also complained about something trivial, perhaps the discomfort of the bed.

We were not a family who wore love on our sleeves – none of that casual "love you" at the end of each phone call. But I suddenly wanted to tell him that I loved him very much. Which I did. And he said the same. I told him I would see him the next day. It was a good conversation somehow.

I flew to Philadelphia and was met at the airport by his carer who was a woman I admired greatly. She clearly adored him, too, and was in a state of some distress. When we got to the airport car park, a complex of buildings all looking alike, she could not find the car. I could see her searching high and low, highly anxious, periodically coming back to apologise. It took an hour, but eventually she found the car and we drove to the hospital.

On arrival, we were informed that my father had died within the previous hour. They took me to him – it was the only time I ever saw a dead body – and he did look strange with all the life taken away. I kissed his forehead and sat with him awhile, but I was exhausted from the trip and also concerned to allow his carer to get home. She drove me back to his apartment and I phoned home to give the news.

Why had he died? The nurse said they never knew why. He had come in with the infection, they were worried about his kidneys, then he started to have a heart attack and they had done what they could. I knew he always said he wanted no 'heroic measures'. But what did it matter why he had died? In retrospect, I wondered whether he had engineered it himself by some not-yet-understood mechanism in order to avoid chemotherapy.

It all happened so fast. But once I had recovered myself, I wanted to thank that young doctor – whose name I never knew – who set up the telephone in the Intensive Care Unit. It had been that special moment at the end.

I was never able to thank him.

Chapter 4: MUCH REMAINS THE SAME: THE PARTS WE LIKE LESS

Introduction

The fact that so much of what we enjoy doing all our lives continues into old age is the good part. But equally, all the things that are most annoying also follow us into our later years. Whatever the new burdens we acquire as we grow older, we do not generally shed those with which we were already familiar. It is simply the other side of the coin.

Again, I write here about some of the things which annoy me, including aspects of my own personality, day-to-day chores and a few odd nuisances. As always, there are numerous others I could have chosen. Other personal qualities that I cannot control. Other people with all sorts of annoying habits from complaining all the time to shouting into their mobile phones. The idea is to show much of our lives continue much as before. You may have a different list.

Again, now and before.

Worrying

I've been a worrier all my life. Some of us are. There is so much to worry about. We can start with the state of the world. At the time of writing, top of the list is the coronavirus, properly known as Covid-19. Everyone is worrying about that. But even before then, there was global warming. Afghanistan. Isis. Korea. Politics of all kinds, whatever political persuasion you happen to be. The list goes on and on. We worry whether the world we are leaving our grandchildren is as good as the world we inherited. And whether there is something more we should be doing about it.

And then there is our immediate family. Children are long the source of worry, when they are small and especially when they are teenagers. At that time, we worried about one thing or another concerning them from the moment we woke up. But it continues when they are grown up. Indeed, if they are married or have a partner, the people to worry about doubles. Does everyone have the right job? Or, for that matter, the right partner? Is everyone coping all right with day-to-day matters, such as getting that possibly dangerous car fixed or are they too obsessed with social media.

People whose adult children have serious problems, such as bringing up a child on their own, a tendency to depression or lack of work, have even more to worry about. I have been fortunate in this respect, but there have been times when one of my grown-up children had a health crisis or a major work concern when I lost sleep thinking about them. You wish there were some way to make it OK, like the sticking plaster you put on their knee when they were children. I am told there is an old Chinese proverb that mothers are as happy as their least happy child. It has a lot of resonance with me.

But worrying also goes down to the grandchildren. Are they getting enough attention from their parents or, perhaps, too much? Is their school giving them the education they need? Do they have enough friends? All the worries that we experienced when our children were small emerge all over again.

And I probably worry about my own self most of all. Nothing heavy, but did I say the right thing to the woman at that event last week? Have I remembered to do that favour for a sick friend that I said I would? Was the person who said they liked my new haircut – or, worse, my latest book – really just being nice? Not to mention all the silly things we inevitably worry about, such as did I remember to turn off the gas when I finished cooking and then went for a walk? Or left a window open where a burglar could see it.

What can we do about all this worry? All my life, people have said to me that I worry too much, that I should relax. Such admonishments annoy me no end. First of all, they won't make any difference. Worrying is part of me. Asking me not to worry is telling me that I should be a different person. At some point, I realised that if worrying is a part of me, I should simply accept it and live with it. I wish my friends would, too. And second, what is worrying 'too much'? Yes, if you are making yourself ill with worry or turning to drink, that is one thing. But worrying too much is also a matter of giving due attention to getting things right. It *can* be a good thing.

Do I wish I worried less? Yes, life would be easier. But it will never change. It is one of those things that has moved with me from childhood through adulthood and now into old age.

Fortunately, I have a husband who hardly ever worries. He says there is no point in worrying about something if there is nothing you can do about it. Since this covers most contingencies, he is a very relaxed man. Sometimes, he points to the spy in Bridge of Spies, played by Mark Rylance, who is constantly asked if he is worried about some major predicament or another.

He always answers, "Would it help?"

The vexed problem of in-laws

It was my last year at university and my English soon-to-be husband had come to stay a few days at our house. My mother, although not keen on the relationship, decided she should nonetheless try to make him feel welcome. Her solution was to buy him some bottled Guinness (England and Ireland got mixed up here) and put it in the fridge, where Americans always keep beer. Being young and not wanting to displease his mother-in-law to be, the poor guy drank the stuff, although he didn't even like it and certainly not cold. Some of it may have quietly gone down the sink when she wasn't looking. This proved, of course, that he liked it. She always had some available when we visited their house. It took some years to put this right.

This story – or its equivalent – gets played out all over the world and, doubtless, throughout time. It arises because of the very strange thing that happens when we marry, our siblings marry or, indeed, when our children marry, namely we acquire in-laws. It can even happen they are simply involved in a close partnership. We suddenly have a lot of new people in our family who we didn't choose, but who we're supposed to love or, at least, be friendly with. And then, there are their parents and sisters and brothers – and their spouses and on it goes.

I have a fairly open-minded disposition, but I am not one of those people who just loves everyone simply because a family member married them. I need to get to know them and determine each relationship for itself. It has been ever thus and will continue to be so. The old mother-in-law jokes were there for a reason. It is primarily because we are supposed to like them – or at least get on with them. Indeed, worse, they are suddenly part of that wider family we are likely to see on special days like Christmas, which may be just the time we want to relax.

Of course, some people are lucky, whose in-laws have delightful personalities, compatible interests and a warm heart. They enjoy each other's company and get together frequently. Indeed, they are truly pleased that someone's marriage or partnership brought them into their life. These are the real winners in life's odd twists and turns. When I interviewed grandmothers for my book on the subject, one woman said that she and her husband went on holiday every year with their extended family of 21 people – four children, their spouses and loads of grandchildren. My jaw dropped at the prospect.

But more frequently, we all just learn to manage. We work out what foods they eat when they come for dinner, what subjects we should avoid in conversations and, best of all, what interests we have in common. In some cases, a genuine sense of warmth develops over time; in others, it remains the sad elephant in the room. Sometimes, we just get our wires crossed as did my mother with her bottled – and carefully cooled – Guinness.

In-laws become particularly important when the grandchildren come along. If we want to see them, the son- or daughter-in-law comes too. They are part of the package. Of course, a baby can be just the thing to cement relationships. The shared love of this new being can paper over a whole lot of cracks. And impressive parenting of the new baby can only help, although arguments about less-than-impressive parenting can work in the opposite direction. I learned a great deal from my interviews with grandmothers about the many ways that new babies could affect inter-generational relationships, including sundering them altogether.

I am not a family expert and have no new insights here. I simply want to acknowledge that one of the key sources of on-going difficulties for many people are new family connections. And while we may complain about a demanding sister-in-law or tiresome son-in-law, we should be careful to reflect on how we, ourselves, are viewed. It may be exactly to us that many less than positive family emotions are directed. Put simply, I may be someone's very irritating mother-in-law.

I even know who the candidates are.

Caring for the sick

Some people are natural carers. They seem to know exactly what a sick or disabled person needs and are ready to provide it. I am not among them. When called upon, I have done my best over the years, for instance when my own children were ill, but I don't think my best is really very good.

I have very limited patience and don't seem to find the right sense of empathy. I try to put myself in their place and imagine what I would want, but I don't seem to succeed. Unfortunately, this is annoying for everyone. Perhaps it is simply that members of my family are both different from me and hard to please.

I first became aware of the existence of family carers when I was relatively young, because my husband's favourite aunt was one. She had found herself in the traditional role (in England) of the youngest daughter who never married, but stayed home to look after her increasingly frail mother. She was not relieved of such responsibilities until her mother died, when she was already in her late forties and rather worn down.

(In her case, perhaps unusually, she blossomed soon after. She married a very nice older widower and began to substitute her previous regular visits to church for equally regular visits to the pub. They moved to a new house and she had a good life for many years until he suffered a stroke and she became a carer all over again.)

I also learned a lot about carers when I was commissioned by a group of organisations to prepare a 'charter for carers' back in the 1980s. I learned about all the ways in which being a carer can be physically and emotionally draining. Not to mention how, once one person accepted the role, others tended to keep away as they saw the 'problem' as solved. Indeed, as in the case of my husband's aunt, it can take over a person's life.

Perhaps I am better at being what I once called a 'semi carer', looking after someone's practical needs at a distance. Until it happened to me, I never thought about the many people who are often caught up in the web created by illness and disability. This awakening came when my daughter-in-law was diagnosed with cancer not long after her baby son was born. (I hasten to say she is fine now.)

Of course, my son had to take on all sorts of responsibilities not normally expected of a young husband and father. But so, too, did many other family members. My husband and I became very active baby-sitters and general helpers-out. We set up our house with all the accoutrements of babyhood – baby bed, highchair, baby clothes, nappies and so forth, so that we would be ready on short notice.

It was tiring and affected all sorts of decisions, such as whether to travel far from home. It wasn't that we were called upon very frequently, but we never knew when it would happen. Whatever our plans for the day, a phone call could arrive at any time asking us to come immediately. I felt my own life was put slightly 'on hold'. When I mentioned the situation to my doctor, he said immediately, "Yes, cancer affects the whole family – that is well known."

In retrospect, it was not difficult to provide the help that we did and being needed to help with a small baby is a mixed blessing. Yes, it created new pressures, but it also brought the pleasures of caring for a baby again. And it made us much closer to that grandchild, which has lasted over the years.

But returning to the present, anyone living with someone in their later years can reasonably assume that they will be needed in this respect, either temporarily or on a long-term basis.

It is not something I look forward to.

Rechnerschmerz

Do not come to visit me when my computer is down. I may snap at you or I may simply say little at all. I lose all sense of proportion and find it hard to think. I might as well be sick. A computer not working is the source of gripping frustration, whether it is the wi-fi connection or the machine itself.

I have long felt that there should be a word for this circumstance. It is like a kind of illness – or, perhaps mental illness. You become irritable, you can't settle, and you can think of little else. You are definitely no fun to be around. It is something to do with the loss of connection to the rest of the world or, even stronger, loss of agency. You want to scream.

It is very different from the breakdown of other appliances. That can be annoying, but it is not in the same ball park. We have experienced a number of such occasions in recent years and they confirm this view. Our dishwasher acquired a mind of its own, with the numbers on the front turning off and on like the lights of a Christmas tree. But we got in an engineer and all was well. Our boiler packed up for a day or two, but again an engineer put it right. Even our telephone handsets began to emit frequent bleeping sounds, but when no remedy worked, I bit the bullet and bought a whole new set of phones.

But the computer is different. You feel it is trying to show you who is boss, not helped by the autocorrect facility which really does decide what word you meant to write. I recently opened my computer only to find that every Excel document was blank. All data gone, from some important statistics to my tally of what I owe my neighbour for some shopping. It then decided that the printer, which had never caused me any problems, had ceased to exist. I could not print a thing. In fear that I was heading for deep trouble, I decided to back it up forthwith, a task I had ignored far too long. But the external disk drive was nowhere to be seen on the desktop when it was plugged in. Nothing much I could do but worry.

Luckily, there is an excellent technical advice service by telephone for this brand of computer and I became very familiar with it. I suspect I will soon be able to recite the number off by heart. Each problem always seems to take at least an hour to resolve, but they do get sorted one by one. Even the lost data was mysteriously restored.

Of course, these are only minor problems next to what a computer can do. The worst, without question, is when it breaks down completely. Nowhere to write down my thoughts (my handwriting is unreadable, even to me), no access to Google to look up information (including a helpline number), no incoming or outgoing emails. Like everyone else, I feel lost altogether when this happens.

After my recent series of computer problems, I decided it was time to find the word for this condition. I wrote to my son, now a university teacher. He was always clever with words and has a number of languages under his belt. I suggested he might combine the word that would have meant computer in ancient Greek if they had such things, with a suitable word for emotional pain or grief.

He replied that the word *hypologistes* in modern Greek means a reckoner and *algia* is the usual ending for pain, like myalgia. So, the word might be something like *'hypologistalgia'*. But he suggested it might be better to go with the German instead and he came up with the word *rechnerschmerz*. *Rechner,* he said, is one word for computer (although modern Germans tend to use the English word computer), and *schmerz* means pain, including emotional pain (as in *weltschmerz*).

Rechnerschmerz – this sounded just right. German sometimes has a way of sounding like its meaning. I now know what I am suffering from.

And so can all the others who undoubtedly suffer the same malady.

Getting down to exercise

Some years ago, one of my grandsons, then age six, really took me aback. "Granny," he asked innocently enough, "would you do me a favour?" I assumed he wanted a second dish of ice cream and said "of course." As one does. "Granny," he continued, "would you and Grandad try really, really hard to stay healthy, because I want my children to know their great-grandparents?" Well, that was surprise. I promised to try. What else could I say?

I eat well and healthily by anyone's standards, but exercise is somewhat harder. We all know that it is important for our health, but how often do we do anything about it? It feels like so much trouble. Once now and again is fine, but doing it on a regular basis is something else altogether. There are so many excuses – a bad night's sleep, someone coming for dinner, we just don't have the energy today. And so forth. The older we get, the harder it is. Believe me, I know.

And yet we all know we should be doing something to keep ourselves in good shape. They keep telling us this. Indeed, we probably all know what might be possible if only we could just get off the sofa and go do it. How can we get the motivation?

First, we need to find something we really like to do. In my case, this was difficult as I had no love of sports throughout my life. And I was no good at any of them – indeed, I was the girl in my PE class who no one wanted on their team. I began to avoid sports wherever possible. Not surprisingly, this continued well into adulthood.

It is easier if there is something you really always liked to do. Playing tennis? Or running? Perhaps just walking. I did love dancing, but it is hard to do on your own and my husband was never interested. In my mid-years, I discovered swimming as one of those things I could tolerate. And even later, I discovered yoga, which I have written about above.

Second, it helps to think about what additional gains you will get from the endeavour. Some people go swimming regularly with a friend and, even if they don't enjoy swimming, they can have a good chat afterwards. I certainly enjoy the camaraderie in my yoga class. I have never forgotten when a fellow follower, in the midst of a particularly arduous (dare I say painful?) stretch, turned to me and said with a wan smile, "It's funny to think that we pay for this!"

Indeed, we often take up exercise to lose a little weight or improve overall body tone. My doctor recommended ten minutes of fast walking every day in order to reduce my blood pressure. I found it had little impact on my blood pressure, but I began to lose weight. This gave me some incentive to continue.

Third, it needs to be convenient. They say that only a small proportion of those who take out membership in a gym actually use it. It may be hard to fit it into the daily routine. My swimming became much more infrequent when the pool I had used was closed down and I had to travel much further to get to one. Strangely enough, when we were all locked in due to the coronavirus, I did more exercise, as I decided to run up and down my stairs once a day. I couldn't possibly say they were inconvenient.

And finally, we all need an extra push. My husband thought up a very novel means to get himself to exercise – he blamed *me* for not nagging him when he didn't. I can now nag with impunity and he is happy. And, when we were locked down, I created a nudge to help both of us do some exercise indoors: I put my yoga mat, (which he also uses), on the floor in the middle of our bedroom.

It reprimands us both as we walk by.

Shopping

I am in a supermarket, standing stock still in front of a shelf full of breakfast cereals. I can't move. I am pondering the right choice. Maybe I should try that one with the little bits of fruit, but no, would I be better off with something with bran? I should check whether there is too much hidden sugar. Or salt. Oh dear, this one is over-priced because it has a child's gift inside. It takes ages. I can't decide. Point a gun and tell me what to choose and I would be much happier.

For me, 'retail therapy' is a contradiction in terms. I have always hated shopping. I occasionally wonder if I had a bad experience in the past and a dose of the right sort of aversion therapy (or is it the opposite?), might change my position. I doubt it. There is very little about shopping I could learn to like.

First, I really hate being given too much choice. Yes, we consumers are supposed to love choice and cereal brands have done a fine job of giving it to us. They are not alone. Everywhere you go, it is necessary to make fine decisions on ingredients or style of a t-shirt or colour of a small rug. And for some items, like house furnishings, you need to get colour and size just right or it is useless. My brain does not cope well. It finds it necessary to consider all the permutations. I become like a deer caught in the headlights.

Secondly, I am really uncomfortable in crowds. I try to find times to shop when the crowds will be small, but it is difficult. Many shops are quiet first thing in the morning, but if it requires public transport to get there, you are stuck in any case. I would never shop in one of those Christmas sales – people struggling to get into the front in order to acquire that one thing specially on sale is my idea of sheer hell.

Thirdly, I can't bear the whole process of trudging from shop to shop to find the right thing. I find it incredibly dispiriting. Leaving aside day-to-day food shopping, I have never found one store – yes, even a large department store – which sold exactly what I wanted in every department. Trudging is the name of the game.

And finally, I am not very acquisitive. I don't much like 'things'. Of course, I need to buy food and other items, but it is much more of a chore than a pleasure. A new dress rarely cheers me up. Nor does finding just the right vase or tablecloth. I might make an exception for a new book I look forward to reading, but there aren't many such exceptions.

Not surprisingly, I am much happier with mail order. It is so easy in this day and age. I have learned, over time, which companies sell trousers that actually fit and which catalogues' pictures are reasonably accurate. Some companies have very helpful staff who will discuss details like the 'feel' of a garment. Much welcomed by me. It is a bit of a nuisance when you need to send things back, but they are making the packaging much more suitable for this purpose. And at least the line in the post office is not much longer than the line in the store you would have experienced if you had bought the item in a store in the first place.

Shopping feels like a kind of test that I am always failing. Either I come back with nothing - and everyone says "What? You couldn't find *anything* you liked?" Or I come home with something and they say "What? You chose *that*?"

I am sure that I will hate shopping until the very end.

Coping with baby photos

It happened again very recently. A friend – a new grandmother – was telling me about her wonderful new-born granddaughter. The baby was all of two weeks old and there really wasn't much to say about her, but somehow conversations in these circumstances manage to continue for some time. And then, the crowning moment, my friend reached into her purse, brought out her phone and showed me pictures. All I could see was a blanket, an enclosing arm and some pinkish flesh where the baby's head must have been. Aside from ethnicity, it could have been any baby, more or less.

All my life, I have just never been one of those women who easily cluck over other people's photos. If you go back far enough, there were pictures of our friends' boyfriends or of their pets or of their baby sister. My thought always was yes, I see them, but what can I say? They look nice enough, but I could never think of the right words. It tends to give you the reputation of being 'cold'. But you don't mean to be.

It gets worse, of course, as we grow older because then we are shown pictures of the wedding or the ring (if you're distant) or, inevitably the husband. I never had much more to say about these. I am just not good at it. But at least pictures in those days were more limited in scale – they had to be taken, developed and collected from the chemist shop or whoever developed them. They seemed prolific, but how could we have known of the tsunami of photos to come?

Meanwhile, as we grow older, we no longer get so many pictures of new husbands or rings, but yes, our friends are, one by one, becoming grandmothers. And grandmothers are probably the worst when it comes to baby pictures. Of course, it is a time of excitement, love and warmth – and they are eager to share this with their friends. And what better way than via pictures of the new baby? It is so easy. Baby born at 2.10 in the afternoon? You can have the picture by 2.15, if not earlier.

Well, I am no better at clucking over photos of new-born grandchildren than I am of new-born children. A real live baby – yes, every time. You can hold them, cuddle them, smell them. But pictures just don't do it for me. In fact, with baby pictures, it is often hard to see anything aside from a tiny face, eyes closed, hardly visible underneath blankets and enfolding arms.

It gets easier as babies gain a few months, because then you can comment on who he or she looks like. "Oh, she's got her father's eyes" can be a genuine response. And you can talk a bit about what the baby is doing, how much sleep the parents are getting and how often the other grandmother sees them. The older, the better.

I have been pondering how there can be such a disparity in the feelings of those showing pictures and those looking at them (or, at least, some of us). What is going on? It is obvious once you think about it. Women showing their grandchild's picture – even the little face hidden in a blanket – imbue the photo with all the love that they feel. They don't see a hardly visible baby – they see the baby they have held and felt so much love for.

The onlooker, in contrast, cannot easily share this, however happy they are for the grandmother herself. They know what their friend is feeling, but cannot conjure up the same senses from a photo. Indeed, one can go further. The same problem can arise with pictures of any new love in a friend's life, for instance a man they have recently met. You can wish them well, but you cannot call up all that emotion in the same way.

Bring on the live babies any day.

The pressure of presents

I have always felt a certain pressure associated with gifts, whether for Christmas or birthdays or any other purpose – and whatever the time of year. I have never much liked giving them, but I also never much liked getting them. They are supposed to be the sign of love or thanks or all kinds of positive emotion, but too often they feel more like a burdensome responsibility.

There is the occasional exception. One is giving presents to children. You know from their parents what they are broadly longing for – and there is such delight when they get it. No problem there. And once in a while, I find myself in a shop, realising that the thing I am looking at is exactly what a friend or relative would treasure. There is again great pleasure in buying it for them, giving them a delightful surprise. Happiness all around.

But more generally it is a different story. You don't know what the recipient will like – certainly not in sufficient detail to buy something for them. And even if you know their taste exactly, you then don't know whether they already have a particular item. One relative loves the novels of a famous writer, but does she have all of his books? Another loves executive toys, but have I seen this one on his desk? One can spend hours pondering over this problem. You end up with the usual bottle of wine or bouquet of flowers. These are, at least, safe.

A different solution is the wish list. At Christmas, my family – and I suspect many others – all have a wish list telling me exactly what presents they would like to receive – which book, which pair of slippers, which annual calendar. Buying these is rather like doing my weekly grocery shop. Check the list, buy, wait for the post. No artistry in this. No surprise when the package is opened. The one benefit is the person will welcome the addition to their wardrobe or library or whatever and won't feel the need to send it back.

It is not only buying presents – I never much liked receiving presents either. As a child, there might be a longed-for item – a special doll or a pretty dress – and when this was given to me, yes, it was pleasing. But most of the time, it was the wrong thing. The grandmother who often spent Christmas with us had good intentions, but was not very good at working out which age was good for which item. More surprisingly, my parents were not much better. Even when I was fully adult, my mother could not resist buying some dress that she thought would "look cute" on me, which was never to my taste.

And the problem is that I have always had a strong aversion to waste in all its forms. The wrong present is a complete waste – a waste of money, a waste of someone's time acquiring it and a waste of any effort I make to wear it or read it or use it however it was intended. A waste and an embarrassment. I say thank-you, of course, but it all makes me very uncomfortable.

But there is one exception. A few years ago, I was quietly working on my computer on a grey afternoon in late November when the doorbell rang. We weren't expecting anyone, so I assumed it was probably one of those charity workers who come along at Christmas time. I let my husband handle it. He shouted up to me that we had a large parcel. I knew we hadn't ordered anything, so I rushed down in the hope I could catch the delivery man before he disappeared. Too late. My immediate thought was it was going to be a nuisance to get this sizeable thing taken back.

But the parcel had my name on it, so I began to investigate. It was a large basket. After removing coloured ribbons and layers of see-through plastic, I realised it was some kind of hamper full of fruit, a variety of chocolates and a bottle of sparkling wine. What a nice thought on someone's part, even if it was surely not intended for me. But there was a note, addressed to me, from my lovely neighbours who were temporarily away, thanking me for looking after their house. It was for me, after all. A complete surprise on a grey day.

A present I liked – not a waste at all.

How difficult can it be to buy a mop?

I suspect everyone feels that they spend too much time on life's trivia, whether they are 24 or 74. It continues right on up. We all know the sort of thing – dealing with gas or electricity bills, ensuring the right basic food staples are in sufficient supply or just keeping the household running day-to-day. A certain amount of time is acceptable, but sometimes there is a problem that refuses to be fixed easily. You try one thing, then another and nothing works – and you end up having a very bad day.

This happened to me recently when I needed to buy – of all prosaic things – a mop. The mop handle broke, in just the same way its predecessor had done before. I decided I not only needed a new mop, but perhaps a new *kind* of mop. I asked my very savvy neighbour what mop she would recommend. I won't bore anyone with the details, but she suggested a particular type and brand (it was a mop and bucket set) and I thought the problem was solved. All I needed to do was to buy it.

I am a great believer that you can buy anything online and very quickly. I went to the online supermarket that I use regularly and could see no sign of this mop. Yes, they had the bucket, they even had refill mops for this brand, but the mop itself was nowhere to be seen. So off I went to the famous online purveyor, named after a large South American river, the supplier that everyone loves and hates at the same time. Yes, they had the mop, but not the bucket. I was informed that they would have the perfect 'mop and bucket set' in three weeks, even at a good price. But I wanted the mop now. This was getting annoying.

I then remembered that there is a not-too-distant hardware store, which sometimes has such things as mops, although it tends to be overpriced. I phoned to check. They had the mop, but the price given was so low that I doubted if it was the right one. And the bucket would be just under £50 ($65). I even phoned back to see if I got that right. Was it a silver-plated bucket? I have no idea, but I do not need a bucket for that price!

This was now getting seriously annoying. I was definitely losing my sense of proportion and needed to stop. I went off to make lunch. This may have been a mistake. I began to do stupid things with the stove. I certainly managed to annoy my long-suffering husband, who said he thought I was about to burn myself or even damage the house, never mind the lunch. I didn't. But it was not a relaxed time. I kept trying to explain what a problem I had had, but he said he wasn't really interested in a mop. Conversation came to a stop. And, indeed, who could blame him? How interesting can a mop be?

After this break, I worked it out. I bought the mop from one online store, which arrived the next day, and ordered the bucket from the other, with some other groceries, all of which were duly delivered a few days later. That was that – a shiny new mop and bucket set.

Why do we get so annoyed at such trivia? Is it just me on a bad day? No, I think little things can set anyone off from time to time. And the fact that it is a small thing just makes it worse. You know you should 'do better' when the issue isn't all that serious. I wondered whether it is the internet. I doubt it, but it does raise our expectations that everything is available quickly. And things often are. We need to learn that 'often' isn't 'always' and build it into our planning.

Think of our mothers – or, even more, our grandmothers – who would never have had the luxury of dealing with such trivia so quickly. They would have needed to trudge down to actual shops, often some distance away, to find what they wanted, if they found it at all.

They would be amazed to see how easy it is for us today.

STORIES FROM MY LIFE

Rolling pin man

2000

I was told that jury service is inevitably boring. Not mine. It was fascinating, haunting, very absorbing and probably a lot of other emotions combined. But never boring. By total chance, I ended up on the jury for a murder trial – one so sensational that it was being reported in the daily newspaper.

I presented myself, as asked, at the Westminster Crown Court on a Monday morning in June. My name was called for a jury just after lunch. I was asked a series of questions, especially about any contacts with Westminster University. It turned out that I was a replacement juror, as one had just been dismissed because of such a connection. I was quickly ushered into the trial room, where everyone seemed glad to see the end of a long wait and the trial got under way immediately.

The atmosphere was very intimidating. It was the trial of a research assistant in the Psychology Department of the University, named Stephen Reid. He fully admitted to having killed a young computer advisor, who had been very kind to him in the course of her work with him. He had killed her with a rolling pin ("Rolling pin man", shouted the headlines), because he intended to commit suicide and wanted to take someone nice with him into 'the afterlife'.

But Reid had declared diminished responsibility due to mental health problems. The purpose of the jury, we were told, was to decide not his guilt, but whether his mental health problems were so severe that by law he had diminished responsibility. He would be locked away in either case, but our verdict would determine whether he would be sent to a standard prison or a psychiatric hospital. This was a Kafka-esque situation. A jury is not comprised of mental health professionals. How were we supposed to determine the correct answer? But we well understood our responsibility both to the accused and to his victim.

Four psychiatrists had examined Reid. Three had declared that he suffered from schizoid personality disorder; the fourth had initially concurred, but then changed his mind. This left us with a dilemma. Should we interpret this to mean that the last one was very uncertain – or that he was highly certain, as it must take considerable courage for a professional psychiatrist to change his mind.

The trial lasted the better part of a week. We were shown gruesome pictures of the dead woman – a pretty, bright and talented Cambridge graduate from London. We were taken through Reid's life from an unhappy childhood in the North of England to a loner academic in London. He was that colleague (does every workplace have one?) who everyone thought should be offered some friendliness, but no one wanted to be the one to do so. He clearly worked hard both at his paid research and on his own PhD, had no friends and was not very easy to talk to. He was described as having "low social skills." This, I suspect, was an understatement.

We were also taken through the period before, during and after the murder in some detail. The most striking factor to me was that Reid was working on two distinct emotional levels at the same time. For instance, the day before the murder, he handed out questionnaires to students in a busy classroom as part of his ongoing PhD research, and immediately went out to a local department store to buy the rolling pin, adhesive tape and other materials which he intended to use for the murder.

The murder itself had gone wrong in just about every way. The young woman had proved harder to kill than he expected, making it a very messy business, although he succeeded in the end. He had then fled to a cheap hotel and taken pills to kill himself, but vomited them up. He then fled to Brighton and tried to hide out there, but was recognised and arrested some ten days later.

We have all watched TV dramas where detectives tape record discussions with a witness, announcing the time and who is present. In court, these transcriptions were read out at length. What was most astonishing was Reid's complete lack of emotion. He carefully described his plans and procedures for the murder and the period afterwards, but with absolutely no remorse. There was no, "Oh my God, I don't know what got into me, how could I have done that?" He was just very straight – and very, very cold.

Which leads me to the most memorable part of the whole experience – the chilling nature of being around a person lacking any emotion. My jury seat happened to be closest to the place where Reid sat in the courtroom and it was as if he were radiating a lack of human affect. He sat passively, with virtually no expression, occasionally passing a note to his counsel.

I felt the chilling quality of his persona from the first day and throughout the trial. I found it incredibly disturbing, but also somehow fascinating. It was so terrible, it was almost moving. Indeed, once the trial was over, I contacted a psychiatrist I knew through my work to discuss my reaction. He confirmed that the experience of someone with schizoid personality disorder could be very distressing, even for professionals working with them.

I am not allowed by law to discuss the jury deliberations, nor how we reached a verdict, but I can say that the jury members were, almost uniformly, very impressive. We spent five very intense days going over the information, arguing back and forth. I felt like I was in the movie *Twelve Angry Men* and several others said they did, too. The whole experience was very tiring and haunting. I found myself dreaming about it.

Eventually, we determined by ten to two (as allowed by the judge) that the killer did suffer sufficient mental health problems to accord him diminished responsibility. Our foreman duly reported this to the court, the judge accepted the verdict and said that sentencing would take place one month later. We were dismissed.

We said our goodbyes and literally disappeared into the crowd on a sunny afternoon. It felt anti-climactic after such an intense period.

About a month or so later, I read in the newspaper that the judge determined, against the jury's advice, that Reid did not have diminished responsibility and he was sent to an ordinary prison. One had to question why we had spent all that time and effort.

I have wondered from time to time whatever happened to Stephen Reid. I assume he worked on – and possibly completed – his PhD, in prison. He must have been let out by now, but my limited internet searches have revealed nothing.

Perhaps he has changed his name.

Birth Day

2006

They say that mothers forget giving birth, a trick of Mother Nature so that we will be happy to have more babies. I do remember the birth of both my children pretty well, but whether I fully remember the pain I cannot say. (I do remember the pain of a kidney stone, when I was only 22, to this day and would swear that it was worse than childbirth, despite the lack of any ready method of measurement.)

What I do remember very vividly was the birth of my first grandchild. My daughter had an extremely long period of labour – over a period of days – and I had gone to her house for some of the time to help out. She was under the care of a team of highly respected independent midwives who, in retrospect, should have sought medical care much sooner. But all went well in the end.

There had even been talk of a home birth, a surprise to me, but the long labour put paid to that idea and she was eventually admitted to hospital. Her husband was with her there and I joined them, as she had asked, as the labour progressed. I found myself pacing up and down like the proverbial father-to-be. You just know – perhaps more than you did when you were younger and less experienced – that things can go wrong. In my case, this was not helped by the fact that a friend's sister had – one month before – encountered major birthing difficulties, resulting in permanent disability for her baby daughter.

I found that the sound of the baby's heartbeat over a monitor, which should have been reassuring, was incredibly frightening. I kept thinking that the beat I just heard might be the last. I worried both for my daughter and for the baby. Indeed, I worried so much I began to wonder whether I was becoming a problem.

And it is the only time I have ever witnessed a crash team. One minute everything was carrying on as normal and another, after some signal that I hadn't even noticed, there was a rush of movement and a perfect triangle of five or six hospital staff. It was frightening and impressive at the same time.

At the last minute, my daughter was found to need a caesarean and her husband was, quite reasonably, so exhausted from the long labour that he was worried he might faint in the delivery room. We had not discussed the possibility, but I offered to take his place and, with a look of great relief, he quickly agreed. I held my daughter's hand as they prepared her for the procedure, asking every two minutes when they were going to put up the curtain.

It is such an intimate time, I felt enormously close to her, of course, and pleased that I could help at this momentous hour in her life. And my reward was that when my grandson was duly born, he was immediately placed into my arms. She didn't have the strength to hold him at that moment and the father was outside. But we called him in and they were both holding their new son very soon. I stayed with them awhile and it was after midnight that my son-in-law drove me to a point in central London where I could get a taxi home.

I have no original words to describe the special quality of birth. It means a new life for the grandchild, of course, but it also means a new life for everyone around the baby – his mother, his father and many others yet to come. Not to mention the grandmother.

I remember feeling high as a kite, unable to settle or sleep. I sat up late into the morning sending emails about the birth to various family and friends. I was thrilled to add in the immortal – and incredibly self-important – words of Margaret Thatcher, "We are a grandmother!"

I had been waiting to use those words for years.

Encounter in Rome

2013

It was a longer holiday than we usually took and we had rented a spacious but old flat in central Rome. It wasn't our first visit by any means, but we did many of the usual things – going to churches and galleries, spending a memorable evening in the Vatican and just walking around.

One day, we had gone out for lunch to a rather old-fashioned local restaurant. It had been in the same location for decades, perhaps with the same classic menu and the numerous waiters in black uniforms. I can't remember now what it was called or what we ordered, but the food was reasonably good. The tables were close together by English standards. Our two-person table was next to another, perhaps only an inch or so apart, so they could be easily joined for a group of four. As a result, we became increasingly aware of an older man, perhaps in his eighties, sitting alone at the table just next to ours. He was well dressed, with a confident air and an intelligent face. He seemed to be known to the restaurant staff.

We had been married for fifty years and had a very easy way of chatting about all kinds of things, from what we had been seeing in Rome to our grandchildren, the current news and much else besides. I wondered how much this man could hear of what we said, but nothing was so confidential that it mattered much. Sometime after we had finished our second course and were ordering coffee, he made eye contact with us. He offered a comment about the food or the restaurant or something similar of no great importance. He spoke in good English, although it was clearly not his native language.

But this had broken the ice. He asked where we were from. When we said London, he told us that he loved London, especially the gentlemen's clubs around St James. This was not part of our world, but we smiled to be agreeable. He mentioned that one of his sons worked in England and he liked to visit from time to time.

He then told us he was from a South American country (unnamed here to preserve his anonymity) and was a former Supreme Court judge there. I wondered briefly if I should believe this, but decided it was an unlikely detail to invent. He had been forced out when the then president came to power and he had moved hurriedly to Europe. Most of his time was spent in Rome, but he travelled around to England and other countries.

There was some mention of a wife and four or five grown up children, but it did not sound like he had much contact with them, even his wife. Indeed, he seemed a slightly forlorn figure, eating alone – most likely frequently – in a foreign city.

He asked about us. How long had we been married? Did we have children? What were we doing in Rome? All reasonably innocuous. Most of this was directed to my husband, possibly because he was more comfortable talking man-to-man or perhaps simply because the configuration of our seating meant that he was more within direct eye-contact.

And then suddenly the conversation took a very different turn. He said it looked like we loved each other very much and stopped briefly to check for confirmation. My dear husband, although normally reticent like most Englishmen, said yes, we did. I think I nodded or murmured some agreement.

"Would you mind my asking," this stranger began, "but what do you mean by love?"

The atmosphere shifted. This was not a light-hearted question, but a serious question from a serious man. We knew it, he knew it and he knew we knew it. Perhaps he was trying to work something out in his own mind. I could see my husband beginning to reflect, to search for an answer. "That's a difficult question," he said, buying a little time. "Yes," was the quiet reply. My husband is a reflective man and not afraid of difficult questions. As an academic, he is used to them. But this was definitely not part of his lunch plans.

"Well," he began, "looking back I'm not at all sure that I was in love when we first married. Of course, I was strongly attracted for many reasons, but I didn't understand then what love was. I was much too young and un-formed. And my mind was on other things – mostly myself and where I was going. Had I been asked what love meant, my answer would probably have focused on my wife's special qualities."

"But," he continued, "I feel now that love is something that develops slowly over time. It requires a period of growing into maturity. If I had to define it, it's something to do with wanting what is good for my wife – to be willing, if necessary, to sacrifice my own interests in order to help her. Of course, I may also benefit from doing that, but I would do it even if I didn't. I want – very deeply – for her to be happy and fulfilled. It's in this same way that I also love my children and grandchildren."

All of this was said quietly over some time in a slow and thoughtful way.

I'm not a weepy person nor a sentimental one. I don't weep in the opera or when watching a touching movie. But here was my husband trying to explain his love for me, right in the middle of a public restaurant in Rome. My eyes definitely misted up. There was nowhere, anywhere, except these two small tables.

My husband said later that the judge's eyes were also moist. He had looked lost in thought, perhaps seeing what might have been absent from his own marriage. The table became rather quiet. The judge said something to the effect that he wasn't sure he had ever experienced this. We slowly went back to more normal conversation.

At some point, the waiter came for the bills and they were paid. "This has been a very interesting discussion," the judge said. We could have taken contact details and continued the conversation elsewhere – after all, he said he came to London from time to time. But I made a calculation that we were not likely to have that much in common and a future relationship was unlikely to thrive. Perhaps he thought so, too.

We shook hands and left the restaurant separately.

We didn't even know his name.

Chapter 5: AND, WITH A LITTLE BIT OF LUCK, THERE ARE SURPRISING NEW JOYS

Introduction

And here is the good part. Yes, growing older has many very visible drawbacks, from increasing wrinkles to new illnesses and new things to worry about. Yes, many of the irritations experienced throughout life continue to annoy us. That territory has been well covered here and elsewhere.

But our later years also bring many compensations – and it is important to celebrate them. For a start, for many of us, there are grandchildren. Not everyone has them, of course and – worse – some who have them cannot enjoy them because of the exigencies of distance and uneasy family relationships. But in the great majority of circumstances, these little beings bring a new and heightened meaning to our lives. And at the same time, other relationships often strengthen and thrive — whether with a partner, adult children or long-held friends.

But our older years are also enhanced by a new sense of ourselves. It can take a lifetime for some of us to really understand and accept our own strengths and weaknesses, not to mention any unsung contribution to those around us.

Yes, some do so long before, but it is a time of coming to terms with ourselves, bringing a greater sense of inner peace. This, to me, is the real bonus of later life.

Lighting up all over

Ask almost any woman about her new grandchild and she will light up all over, like a young woman in love. It was certainly true for me. Grandmothers are invariably thrilled to bits. Grandfathers, too. Perhaps that is all we need to know. We have become grandparents and we love it. But for those with a naturally enquiring mind, an interesting question is – why? What is it about this new-found role that is so fulfilling? There are many answers.

Let us start with the grandchildren. Of course, we adore them in all their different shapes and sizes. Some remind us of our own children – their parents – and feel we are living our earlier lives all over again. Some are completely different and we cherish the novelty of their interests and personalities.

And it is fun to do things with them – to dandle a new baby on our knee, to get down on the floor and do puzzles with a toddler, to take children to the park. Loads of activities which we did a myriad of times and thought we might never do again. Indeed, perhaps we got fed up then – oh dear, do I really need to read this story again? But now we have time and we see the intrinsic pleasures much more readily.

And if one is an instinctive teacher, it is wonderful to teach them about the world. They have so much to learn and we have so much to give. Whether this is a matter of explaining hard facts, like the names of flowers, or offering some form of guidance about how to cope with teenage problems, there is a deep satisfaction in the process. It is extraordinarily fulfilling to be able to offer new little beings your hard-won wisdom.

But having grandchildren is much more than that. It means that our children will have all the joys of parenthood. We have always wanted the best for them and, perhaps, spent hours talking about what they want to do with their lives. We also know that having children helps both men and women to learn and grow into themselves. It is something we may well have wanted for our sons or daughters for some time, whether we explicitly thought about it or not.

And finally, the part of being a grandparent that is perhaps the most surprising is what it does for us grandparents ourselves. Yes, it is fun to play with the children, yes, we want our children to be fulfilled – but there is something more than that. Having grandchildren does much deeper things.

Many people feel that they were not the best of parents – perhaps they were just too young and inexperienced. Or perhaps they were too involved with their work or other issues. Having grandchildren provides an opportunity to do it again, to do it better and, in some small way, to make amends. It is that rare thing in life – a second chance. I know I felt this way.

As we grow older, we begin to think a little more often about the longer term. Has our life been worthwhile? Have we left something good behind? Grandchildren necessarily represent the future – and it may be they will remember us over time. We like to think that perhaps there will be a conversation, twenty or thirty years hence, that begins "I remember my grandma telling me...."

A corollary of this thought is the passing on of our genes. Some people don't think this is very important, and that is fine. Indeed, I am one of them. But some get great pleasure from seeing the same shock of red hair that had not shown up in the family before now or, indeed, the same fascination with mathematics.

And finally, most surprising of all, is that the fact that we like ourselves so much better when we are with our grandchildren. It is such a wonderfully innocent relationship, not full of the constant anxieties that beset parenthood. You can relax and just be yourself. It's not something we think about a lot, but if we do, we might realise that it is very self-affirming.

I was so fascinated by the complexities of being a grandmother that I wrote a book about the subject, based on interviews with a wide range of women in terms of their backgrounds and experiences. It is called *Celebrating Grandmothers*.

Even after writing a whole book, I still find the subject fascinating.

Better than being a parent

I learned the quote years ago, but I didn't truly understand the meaning. I had to look it up to check. I thought it might have been Groucho Marx who said, "The best reason to have children is in order to have grandchildren." No, it seems to have been Gore Vidal (of all unlikely people) who wrote, "Never have children – just grandchildren!" And Lois Wyse, a prolific American author, wrote, "If I had known how wonderful it would be to have grandchildren. I'd have had them first!"

Any grandparent would readily 'get' these quotes. When we have grandchildren, especially if we see them fairly frequently, we tend to develop a special bond with them. Not inevitably, but it is very common. Certainly mine. Which made me wonder why being a grandmother is so much easier and fun than it ever was being a mother.

There are a lot of answers. Grandmothers themselves often comment on how they get the best of both worlds – they have the fun of having children around, but also the relief – that parents don't have – of being able to hand them back at the end of the day. Yes, hooray to that. Long days with small children are tiring at any age, but especially as we grow older. All we want is to lie down or pour ourselves a glass of wine. Perhaps both.

But frequent as this is as an explanation, I don't really think it is the main story. Others say that the real reason grandchildren are so enjoyable is that we can be much more generous with them, even indulgent. It is fun to give small children a little extra pleasure, such as that extra piece of cake, in a way we would never have done for our own children. Back then, we felt much too responsible for giving them the right attitudes and self-discipline.

And, indeed, discipline is the other side of the coin. We were always on the alert to teach our children how to behave, to be aware of the consequences of their actions or simply just to display good manners. If they did not behave as we thought they should, it was down to us to set it right. As grandparents, we don't feel this need so strongly. Some of us may want to teach good values and attitudes to our grandchildren, but we know it is not our responsibility. We may well try to fit in with the values of the parents, but for the most part we can relax.

Indeed, there is more. We are older and may think we have gained some wisdom during the decades since we were parents. And we probably have. Moreover, because we are often retired, we are not so beset with other demands, such as work to be completed for a particular deadline. We can relax. And this means we can stop and enjoy these children to the fullest. Some of us did so the first time around (with our children), but many of us did not succeed. I know I didn't some of the time.

There is, in my view, a very complex 'virtuous circle', which means that everything improves over time. In the early days, grandparents are usually excited to have a baby or small child in the house again. As noted, they are often more relaxed anyway, being under fewer pressures, and want to please the grandchildren in any way they can. And, as also noted, it offers the chance to 'make up' for their faults as parents. At the same time, the grandchildren come to the grandparents with their good manners — whether by instinct or parental instruction, they know they should behave at their best in other people's houses. They sense the love and the welcome.

This makes for a great start. Both want to please the other, while both feel the other is 'special' because they are family. And because both sides are so easy and comfortable with each other, it just carries on that way, strengthened further by the presence of love. They see us at our best and we see them at their best. What could be better? And there is little or none of the tensions that can quickly develop when things are going wrong at home, whether between the parents or, indeed, between the parents and the children.

As the children grow and develop, they bring their new accomplishments to the grandparents with great pride. And we grandparents respond accordingly. A natural bond is readily sealed by all this love and time. Even when — or perhaps I should say "especially when" — the grandchildren become teenagers and tend to rebel against their parents, our house can be a place of calm. They have no wish to rebel against us.

A lovely example of this happened not long ago. One grandson had just learned to email and started emailing his grandfather. On one occasion, he made a typo, so he accidentally wrote 'frand-dad'. And when he realised this, he said it was a good word, because they were friends as well as grandfather and grandson. He said he would start calling him 'frand-dad'.

Of course, relationships will be different where grandparents see the grandchildren infrequently, for there is so much less time for this bond to develop. It will also be different where grandparents are raising their grandchildren full time, for instance, due to sickness, divorce or other problems in the middle generation. Here, grandparents are acting in the role of parents and may have had to forego the luxury of being grandparents in the way described.

I have frequently heard my children commenting, "My goodness, he behaves so differently in your house," or, "I wish he would act like this at home." We smile and feel innocent and they wonder how we do it.

I do hope that they will learn the secret in the fullness of time.

New little people in our lives

I find that as I grow older, it is harder to make new friends, to bring new people into my life. Yes, it can happen, but the occasions for doing so seem less frequent. Yet with grandchildren, they come ready made. Unlike friends, we didn't choose them for their particular compatibility with our personalities, but this makes it even more interesting to get to know them. I personally find this a constant delight.

Just as with your own children, it takes time to work out who they are. But this gives an extra pleasure to watching them grow into distinctive individuals. One minute, there is a little new-born baby, looking sweet and untouched. Then, in what feels like no time at all, you suddenly have a strong personality. It is quite breath-taking.

I am not an expert on the nature-nurture debate, but it seems to me that babies come out of the womb with many pre-set qualities. We see these emerge over time – and perhaps we affect them somewhat in our upbringing – but I tend to believe that the person was there from the very beginning. We all notice this sort of thing with our own children. One is quieter than other kids – or noisier. Another loves sports or hates them. One is constantly drawing, while a sibling will never touch a crayon. Some listen to what you say – and some never do. The many variations go on and on.

And we have had the pleasure of watching them grow up into adults, often developing and honing the traits they showed as small children. The five-year-old boy who sang at every opportunity develops into a singer of some kind, whether in church or a rock band. The little girl who nurtured her pets with great diligence grows up to become a nurse, or a doctor or a stay-at-home mother. Of course, children can change and you can never be certain how they will develop. But it certainly works with hindsight – how often have we looked at our adult son or daughter and realised how their qualities were there from the very beginning?

It starts all over again with grandchildren. We are probably quicker at spotting their notable characteristics, given our experience. They love to dance or to erect complex towers with wooden blocks or to kick a football. They argue back a lot or go sullen. They are deeply sensitive. Or musical. We notice.

Many of these qualities come out in what children say. We noticed that one grandson was very sensitive to the needs of other people from a very early age. He watched people carefully and seemed to have a natural sense of empathy. It came out clearly when he was only five. A favourite aunt had given him a Christmas present before going away. Later, she asked casually which present he had liked most. Without blinking an eye, he said, "Your colouring book." His mother was astonished – the colouring book, a regrettable duplicate, had been put in a cupboard and not even touched. With such diplomacy, one has to think that this child will do well in life.

Our other grandson is very concerned about precision. He wants to make things very clear and works out the exact boundaries of any statement he hears. Again, this showed itself very early on. We were teaching him, age three, about how to cross a very quiet road, lined with parked cars. Now, we said, "You must look to the left – no cars, good – then look to the right, no cars, good, left again. Now we can cross." Quick as a flash, he said, "No *moving* cars." It took me a minute to realise what he was saying, but he was absolutely right. The street was full of cars.

Both grandchildren have grown a lot older since they were the age of these stories. But the same qualities remain very visible, along with many others.

Unique personalities slowly emerge, like the picture in a jigsaw puzzle.

Changing relationships with our children

Having children, when you come to think about it, is one of the oddest things we ever do. It is an enormous leap in the dark, offering very little control over the outcome. Yet, whatever happens – whether you have a girl or a boy, whether you have twins or more, whether there is some horrendous catastrophe, it affects the rest of your life.

We start with wanting a baby. (I will skip over those who never wanted one in the first place.) People with a number of children already may actually think about wanting an eight-year-old (or another age), but most of us get no further in our thinking than that baby. It may be a sleeping new-born baby wrapped in a blanket or it may be a crawling and laughing baby trying out his or her new capacities, but it is definitely a baby in our thoughts.

You don't hear many people say, "I really want an argumentative teenager in my house," or even a sweet cooperative teenager for that matter. Moreover, I never heard anyone say they want a son or daughter of 36 or 45 or 52, who may or may not be in touch. Human beings are not built to think that far ahead.

Yet that is what we end up with for years and years. Of course, they don't stay the same age any more than we do, but they stay adults and yet remain our children. It's all very strange. We look at them and the image can morph into the same person at age two or ten or twenty in the blink of an eye. And yet this small child who we nurtured now has a beard or grey hair and glasses. Not to mention all the abilities and interests we never could have imagined.

Ongoing relationships vary hugely. Some parents talk to their children every day, no matter how distant or how little news to impart. Some lose touch completely, often with considerable pain on or both sides. But I suspect the vast majority of families remain in contact in some way, at a minimum keeping abreast of major developments and recognising occasions such as birthdays. And I suspect that whatever the arguments that may arise from time to time, these relationships remain important.

There are so many variables that affect our relationships with our adult children. Are our interests and personalities compatible? I don't know how many children 'fall close to the tree', as they say, and continue in the family profession. Carpenter begets carpenter and doctor begets doctor. It probably makes family meetings easier unless carpenter the younger takes up some new fad, with which carpenter the elder has no sympathy. It happens. Then, there is the choice of marriage partner, which can bring us together or drive us apart. I have already noted the complexities of in-laws.

And finally – and perhaps most importantly – there is the arrival of grandchildren. I would guess that this event generally serves to cement relationships with our adult children. At a minimum, it means we see them more often, as if we want to see the children, the adults come, too. Of course, arguments may ensue if we don't approve of how the grandchildren are being brought up. Perhaps they give their children too many things and not enough time. Perhaps they seem too strict and or not strict enough. Whether said grandchildren are cuddly young babies or strapping teenagers, there are plenty of ways in which we may want to help our children to cope. The tricky path is to decide how much to say.

But all in all, I like having adult children, the more adult the better. It is a pleasure to see how they have grown and developed. Their interests may not be your interests, but that just adds another dimension to your life. They keep you in touch with the generations below and probably keep you on your toes. Very occasionally, they may even seek your advice.

I find them a constant surprise.

Stronger friendships

Almost everybody has friends. It is part of life to have them. Some of us have loads and some have very few, but we all know who our friends are. They are people who are not our family, not our neighbours and much more important than acquaintances. We get together with them when we can, we talk in person or on the phone and generally view them as important to our lives.

Friendships are common throughout our lives – from when we first went to nursery school up to old age, some remaining constant year after year and some changing. But it is my suspicion that as we grow older, our friendships grow stronger. Those we have held for a long time must become firmer and closer as we share more of the joys and tribulations of ageing. And even those friends acquired late in life feel important simply because of the greater fragility of older people.

Although there is a single word – friends – we would benefit from making a clear distinction among them. They play very different roles in our lives. Some are people we enjoy doing things with – they provide company, diversion and a chance to explore new things. Depending on our culture, we meet them at the local wine bar, pub or café. We tend to get together for regular activities, perhaps to play tennis or to sing in a choir. They probably share our tastes and are usually fun to be with.

We see these friends a lot, but we often don't really know them very well. We chat about our day-to-day lives, but don't go any deeper. They might even be in the middle of a divorce and not tell us about it. The global pandemic may well have affected such friendships, as it was generally hard to keep in touch during lockdown, because so many venues were closed.

In contrast, there are the friends who provide a sense of intimacy – they are the people we tell our problems to, who understand our character and the deeper recesses of our minds. We may or may not do things with them, but they have an importance well beyond the amount of time we spend with them. We may not even see them for years, but the telephone, email and, nowadays, Skype or Zoom enable us to keep up to date.

These friends are often people we knew in school or college and have kept in touch with over the years. They were there for all the ups and downs of our early relationships, they knew when we were trying to have a baby and followed our career choices and dilemmas over time. But they can equally be people we met through any number of more recent circumstances – perhaps at a dinner or through work activity.

We all have relatively few such friends – perhaps only one or two – but these are people with whom we have a very deep connection. Even if circumstances force us to be out of touch for many years, we know that in the first conversation, we will pick up where we last left off. Somehow, there is no need to explain anything. It is unlikely that any lockdown would seriously affect such friendships, because they are too deep.

These distinctions became clear to me over thirty years ago, when I was doing research on people with learning disabilities (different terms were used then), who were being released from the long-stay hospitals in which they had lived most of their lives. Among those concerned with social policy, there was great enthusiasm for moving them out of an institutional setting and into what was always called 'the community'. They would then be free to do what they liked, when they liked, like other people.

But social workers began to notice that the only people many spoke to in the course of a day were those working in shops. In order to help them to find friends, they set up discos and the like where they could meet others. Their intentions were good, but the effect was limited. How many friends – of either sex – would anyone ever make in the loud surroundings of a disco? My colleague and I wrote a report on the issue, but never knew what happened as a result. I would hope that more imaginative ways were found to help them develop and sustain more intimate relationships.

In my own view, it is the people who provide us intimacy who are the most important in the long run. And it is exactly these relationships which are likely to be strengthened as we grow older. We have the time to nurture such friendships and a growing reflectiveness on what is important in life.

They become especially important when we find ourselves unexpectedly on our own.

Stronger marriage or partnership

We were eating a quiet breakfast. My husband had gone out to buy the newspaper, as he did every morning, and on the way back had encountered our very attractive and friendly neighbour. She had just returned from two weeks with her partner sunning themselves on a beach in Greece. He likes to pay people compliments: "You look like a million dollars!" he told me he had said. And she had beamed. And ten minutes later, across the table, he smiled at me – old and grey-haired and, perhaps, still a bit tired – and clearly wanted to say something nice. "You look...well...you look like *half* a million dollars!" And I laughed out loud. Was that a compliment or an insult? Nothing to do but laugh.

Our marriage or long-term relationship is one of the most important in our lives, but it is also the one for which we reasonably seek most privacy. All I can really know is my own marriage, plus a few glimpses into those of my friends. They are, perhaps unusually, mostly long and mostly good.

What I find surprising is that good marriages get so little attention. There are few movies, plays or books that try to capture this experience. Bad marriages get extensive treatment. We all know the stereotypes. There is the hard-drinking detective, who was once married but never able to form a good relationship for long, perhaps because of the hours he keeps. Or the sour middle-aged woman, whose entanglements have been spoiled by selfish men or her close involvement with her children or job. Even in those stories of single people who manage to surmount the many obstacles and finally settle down with the right person, we rarely see the long-term unfolding of their relationship.

I assume that most people believe that good marriages are boring. People don't want to see movies or plays or read books about them. Tolstoy famously wrote: "Happy families are all alike; every unhappy family is unhappy in its own way." Yes, of course, under this reasoning, we don't want to read further. But is he right?

I am pleased to say that I do have a happy marriage, which has lasted over 58 years and counting. I don't know whether anyone would want to read a book about it, but it is anything but boring. A happy marriage is a special kind of friendship. You can talk together about almost anything at some length. You learn from each other. You enjoy just sitting together doing nothing. Perhaps most of all, leaving aside the unsaid obvious, you have frequent laughs together. After a while, you stop even questioning moving on. It feels completely right.

Roughly twenty years ago, two friends in my choir had decided to get married, but not without the normal set of doubts. The woman took me to one side during the tea break and, believing that I was happily married, asked what made for a good marriage. I was not expecting the question and came up with a fairly dull litany of the things one needs to take carefully. I can't remember the exact details, but I know they were all about avoiding the negative – being sensitive to the needs of the other person, minimising quarrels and the like.

I went home and told my husband of our discussion and he burst into laughter. "No, no – It's much simpler than that," he said. "I just find you enormously interesting." I felt my whole argument collapse. He was completely right to put it that positive way and I had been wrong to do anything else. Indeed, I passed on his wise words to my friend and she said, "Good. I find Dan very interesting." They are still married.

I would hate to be a marriage counsellor. All those grudges and recriminations placed oh so carefully in your lap every day! I think I am like the famous Irishman who, on being asked how to get to a particular difficult-to-find place, said, "I wouldn't start from here." So my counselling advice would start much earlier in the relationship and would be pretty simple. Keep talking to each other. Keep having sex. And find out what makes you both laugh –bowling? drinks in the local pub with friends? Adolescent movies? – and do it now and often. For heaven's sake, have fun.

The real problem with the decision to marry is that it requires making a complete guess about the future. Sure, you get on now (and probably have lust on your side), but how will you both change over the years? Will such changes work to help your marriage or hinder it? And how can anyone possibly know? So, do those of us who find ourselves happily married know how we got there? My answer is probably not. Like many things in life, you think it sounds like a good idea – with the usual doubts popping up somewhere between that decision and its execution – and you take the plunge. You then live a few years and find you are getting on better or at least as well – or worse. You live a few more years and those in the last category have probably parted. And you carry on a while longer.

I find that I am often congratulated on my long marriage, presumably on my ability to have been able to live with one person for so long. I find the comment very strange. Why should anyone congratulate me on a life that is full of love and interest and fun?

My view is that marriage gets better and better. After a while, you know each other pretty darn well. You have had a lot of shared experiences. You have most likely lived through the incredible joys and challenges of children. With luck, you have had a lot of laughs on the way. Somehow, there is no going back.

Why would you want to?

Diminished ambition

It was my mother who noticed it first. She and my father had moved into a new retirement home and, after a suitable interval, I asked what the other people were like. She said old people tended to be very nice, especially men, because they no longer had so much ambition. I can't remember whether she elaborated hugely on the comment, but it made me think.

I tend to feel that ambition, when not taken to extremes, is a good thing. It doesn't matter whether a person's aim is to be the best composer of the age or to reach the top job of his or her company (or the country, for that matter). It makes us work harder at what we do and put real thought into how to do It better. Indeed, although I lack appropriate evidence, ambition of one kind or another is probably responsible for most forms of human progress. We seek to get there, so we seek new solutions. We often find new problems as we do so and seek solutions for them. And so forth and so on. Progress gets made.

But the difficulty arises from the unintended consequences of ambition. It drives us on, but it also drives us to neglect other aspects of our lives. Not in every case, but often. Hence, the large number of unhappy wives – or, I hasten to add, husbands – and neglected children. Not to mention the good friends never made. It is all well known. You have heard it all before.

Ambition also tends to drive us to want to be *seen* as successful. Of course, there are people everywhere who quietly succeed in their endeavours without any need to blow their own trumpet. But it is not the most common pattern.

And this makes for a heightened emotional atmosphere much of the time. It is not simply a quiet barbecue among friends – it is a chance for each successful person to let the others know about the triumphs in their lives. The same goes on at dinner parties or down at the pub. It is human nature to let others know. Again, you have heard it all before.

But what happens when ambition dries up or simply comes to a natural end? You composed that amazing symphony or made it to the top of the greasy pole. Perhaps there is another symphony to be written or another pole to climb. But eventually, whether satisfied or not, you reach the point where you slow down or stop altogether. You look around and start to think about other things and other people. And, alongside such changes, you probably become nicer.

Niceness is an under-rated virtue. The very word somehow implies something innocuous and uninteresting. We value it in our friends, of course, but it is rarely on the top of the attributes we commend in people. We tend to note their talents or their achievements and niceness is seen as an add-on, something that comes along with other attributes. But the older I get, the more I see the importance of this quality – it represents thoughtfulness, kindness and a willingness to go the extra mile. It does not bring any kudos, but it makes the world a so much more agreeable place.

My parents' retirement home was full of professional people. There were said to be 17 former doctors, including three or four brain surgeons. There were former journalists, former teachers and, surprisingly, quite a few moderately successful artists. But the emphasis was on the word 'former'. Yes, some of the writers were still writing and some of the artists were still painting, but on the whole, they had moved on. And in the course of doing so, they had become just 'people'.

Once ambition is removed from a person's thinking, the landscape changes. Other people are not some form of competition, but just someone with whom to complain about the terrible weather. You share a beer or a glass of wine and talk about football or the book you are reading. Even when you talk about more contentious issues, such as politics, it is other people's success or failure you are talking about. It is a big change!

So one of the real joys of growing older is the diminishing ambition of everyone you meet. Yes, people still complain. Yes, people still talk about themselves, whether their own latest health crisis or their excitement over a new grandchild.

But it is so restful when the matter of status has been removed.

Being happy in our own skin

An old friend and I were chatting via email. She had sent me a photograph she had taken of me earlier that day. I replied that it made me notice how very white my hair is. It also reminded me that I am not as slender as I used to be. She replied immediately to say I was "beautiful." Which I am definitely not. It came to me that she thought I was one of those women who don't much like their own body and was seeking to reassure me.

I wrote back to say I have never felt ugly nor beautiful, but 'pretty enough' and it was not an issue for me. And she replied, "a rare and precious quality – being happy in your own skin." This stopped me in my tracks. Am I truly happy in my own skin? Is it, indeed, a rare quality?

Of course, this has many meanings, but let us start with the physical one. For as long as I can remember, it never occurred to me to feel that my face or body were not good enough. Yes, I was very short, but that was incapable of being altered (aside from wearing high heels). But I didn't feel the need to 'fix' my body in some way. I never even liked wearing make-up and, after a few inelegant efforts, gave that up. I was – and have remained – a walking WYSIWYG (What You See Is What You Get, a term generated in the computer world).

It was only when I got into my twenties or so that I discovered this was not the case for all women. Many seemed to feel their breasts were too large or too small, their backsides were too big, their noses not the right shape and so forth. And thus, of course, the business of make-up was born (going back to Egyptian times, if not earlier) and, more recently, plastic surgery. Much is the advice given about how to alter physical appearance, both of women and, increasingly, men – getting your hair the right colour, doing the odd nip or tuck and certainly applying loads of stuff to your face. Even the right colours to wear for you. But does it make you happier or, indeed more "happy in your own skin"? I do wonder.

And deeper down, feeling happy with yourself is much more than your physical appearance. Do you like yourself? Do you think people like you? Do you feel you have done enough to meet your early expectations of yourself?

Our initial view of ourselves must come from somewhere. This may be what our parents told us or how we compared to our siblings. Much labelling goes on within families "he's the sporty one" or "she's good with people" and this must rub off. On the other hand, it may not be fully accurate. I was the middle child of three, with the other two being outstandingly clever. Despite reasonable grades in school, it took me years to realise I was really quite bright as well. It hadn't seemed so, by comparison, in my formative years.

Our view also comes from our classmates, not only from those many years of school, but also if we went to university and beyond. We may get a reputation for studying or partying or being thoughtful. We may have loads of friends or very few. We try somehow to work out who we are and what we are good at. And how much do certain qualities and skills matter – to us or anyone else?

And many a novel has been written about the rest of life! It has a way of throwing you a hand-up or pushing you down. It goes without saying that an abusive partner is very likely to flatten self-confidence, just as a quiet but admiring one will do the opposite. Success in work is much the same. It is all part of the process of learning.

On reflection, I feel learning to be "happy in your own skin" is a lifetime's work, at least it has been for me. It is one of the joys of growing older that year by year, you settle in, come to terms with your strengths and weaknesses and accept yourself in a quiet way. You have achieved certain goals, but perhaps not others, and – it is hoped – accept your life for what it has been.

I learned recently of a quotation from David Bowie: "Ageing is an extraordinary process where you become the person you always should have been." Perhaps that is another way of saying the same thing. It all has to do with your personality, your interests, your character and your experience all coming together in one place.

And the important thing is that you view yourself not on the terms of your parents – or your friends or colleagues – but on your own. You tend to care much less about what other people think or say about you.

This is one of the most wonderful bits of being old that people don't tell you about.

A new freedom

It was a few years ago, long before anyone had heard of Covid-19 or face masks. I was walking in the high street on a sunny day in mid-December. I went up to a young couple sitting on a low wall and playing with a toddler, clearly taking a short break from Christmas shopping. Bold as brass, I ventured, "Excuse me. Might you like a book about grandmothers to give to one of your mothers for Christmas?

I have written one...and it's not expensive" – and I showed it to them. "Excellent idea," the man responded and turned to his partner. "Your mother would love it." I gave a reduced price, they were happy and I had a sale. I would never have dared to do that when I was young.

Perhaps the jewel in the crown of growing older – for those of us who weren't clever enough to discover it earlier – is a wonderful sense of freedom from all the unspoken rules by which we have otherwise lived. I don't know why it takes until you are in your later years to come to this conclusion, but I note that it does. Many people say so. Especially women.

The common cliché is that we want to grow old disgracefully. Well, yes and no. A few people actually do – they take to drink or drugs or rock and roll. But most of us simply make little changes to the way we lead our lives that give us pleasure and, perhaps, a sense of relief. They are not disgraceful in any meaningful sense. They just let us express ourselves more truthfully. Some friends or acquaintances may be embarrassed, but in most cases, they wouldn't even notice.

The social rules by which we tend to live are not stated anywhere at all, but we tend to follow them almost as if they were. You may have always felt uncomfortable at parties, but nonetheless, when your good friend invited you to her party, you went. Not only that, you may have bought a special dress, perhaps even shoes, that you didn't really want. And you turned up at the allotted time with a smile. Even worse, you stayed until it was a suitable time to leave.

Older people increasingly say, "The hell with that!" My friend will perfectly well understand that I don't like parties and, while she may miss my presence, she will accept that I am uncomfortable there. Your partner may go or not, as he wishes. You stay home with a glass of wine and a good book. You are free.

Or perhaps you never liked the same sort of movies as your husband, but went along to be sociable – and vice versa. As you grow older, you are more likely to say you will go to what you like by yourself and he can choose his own. What does it matter if you don't go as a pair? You both get what you like and go when you want. You are free.

The same is true for how we present ourselves. People want to look 'smart' or 'casual' or whatever the occasion calls for. I am told that mothers even think about what to wear at the school gates, although I must admit the thought never crossed my mind. Now is the time to do what you like. Buy that supposedly unsuitable leather jacket. Or take to wearing a hat if you always wanted to. Or short skirts. Nobody really cares anyway.

Many of us are told from day one not to talk to anyone we don't know and, although important advice for small children, it remains the social norm in many places. I am a sociable sort wherever I am, so I increasingly talk to complete strangers – at the bus stop, in the supermarket queue or even in the street. Unfortunately, much less during the Covid period, if only because it is hard to make personal contact through two masks. When I used to sell the occasional book to complete strangers in the street, it was always to the utter embarrassment of my family. But what does it matter? No one had to buy.

None of these particular examples are of any great importance in themselves, but they are indicators of a broader state of mind. At some point, we older people feel a sense of liberty to say what we think and do what we wish. Some younger people do, too, but the tendency grows with age. Often, our decisions are perfectly normal within anyone's set of unwritten rules, but sometimes they are not.

This is nothing dramatic. We have not been let out of jail or suddenly found ourselves with enough to eat when we lacked it before. The word 'freedom' has many meanings and I don't mean to compare our lives with other more obvious sources of serious constraint. But small unspoken changes are nonetheless important to us.

They offer a wonderful new lease on life.

STORIES FROM MY LIFE

Traitor

2015

The biggest problem is the pronouns. When you are born in one country and live in another, who do you belong to? When I first met my English husband, we could joke about our respective countries – the horrendous over-cooking of vegetables by 'his' fellow countrymen or the emphasis on hamburgers by 'mine'. Many a time we had a laugh at the expense of the other, generally with good humour.

And then we went to live permanently in London. For a while, the same applied. England was not my country and I was not English. No pronoun problem. But the longer I lived here, the greater the difficulty. I began to talk more frequently about Americans as "them", although I had real problems describing the English as "us." Essentially, I was torn – I felt less and less like an American, but I also did not, 'in myself' as the English say, feel English.

Nationality is a matter of paperwork, but it is also often a matter of heart. As an English politician once posited regarding immigrants, when your two countries are playing, the ultimate test is which team do you root for? For years, I had never thought about my citizenship very much. I was an American by birth and that was that. But I also did not have any great sense of loyalty. I did not feel pride in the American flag or other accoutrements of citizenship. It was just something I was and seemed immutable. Wherever my heart belonged, it did not involve my nationality.

It all began with my decision to undertake a 'junior year abroad' in the academic year 1961-62. While most American students at that time did so at the Sorbonne in Paris, I concluded I would not be able to study political theory in French as it was hard enough in English. I therefore chose to attend the London School of Economics (LSE), where I met my now husband, an Englishman then finishing his degree. Although we subsequently lived in the US for six years during the 1960s, in 1968 we decided to return to the UK. By very good fortune, he was offered a lectureship at the LSE and we have remained in London ever since.

At some point, mainly for the convenience of travelling into the UK when we had been abroad, I decided to take British citizenship. The final straw was a wait of over an hour at Gatwick Airport in London after a plane trip of only forty-five minutes from Amsterdam. At the time, acquiring UK citizenship was neither difficult nor expensive. I did not give it much thought. My US citizenship was not remotely compromised, which was fine. It seemed potentially beneficial to have dual nationality.

But eventually, when it became clear I would never wish to return to live in the US, the disadvantages of my US citizenship began to press. These derived mainly from the fact that all US citizens living abroad were taxed – not only did I not want to incur heavy taxes, but the tax forms were seriously aggravating. Every year, I would say to myself that it couldn't be as bad as I remembered, but I was always wrong. It took the better part of a day.

The wish to renounce their citizenship was growing among many Americans living abroad, but it was highly complicated. The rules and regulations made anyone pondering the idea feel like a traitor. For years, you had to have a good reason to be renouncing (tax was not allowed as a reason) and there were costly penalties. Some specialist lawyers were making sizeable sums. I left it for a long time.

Eventually, I decided to take the plunge and it was incredibly bureaucratic. The restrictions had been eased to the extent that there was no requirement to state a reason for renouncing citizenship. On the other hand, the price had gone up steeply (from roughly $400 to $2300) and the cost of lawyers had similarly risen. The paperwork was horrendous. When I eventually took the pile of packages (the numerous forms were addressed to different states), I was appalled that I needed to pay over £60 just in postage. It was kind of the final nail in an altogether unpleasant coffin.

But the 'fun' part, if there was one, was the actual date of renunciation. I had to go to the US Embassy, through enormous security, and wait my turn. I was called to a window, where I first had to hand over my credit card for payment, and then swear an oath. The first part of this was in the usual bureaucratic language of the section of the Immigration Act pertaining to the matter and then continued:

> "I hereby absolutely and entirely renounce my United States nationality together with the rights and privileges and all duties and allegiance and fidelity thereunto pertaining. I make this renunciation intentionally, voluntarily, and of my own free will, free of any duress or undue influence."

I was certain there was a fair amount of redundant verbiage in the last sentence. As an editor, I would have happily pointed this out. As an almost no-longer-US citizen, I decided this would not be advisable. I walked out of the US Embassy feeling a free woman.

But I still have problems determining the correct pronoun.

Dégâts des Eaux

2018

I am somewhere warm, friendly, sensual. Not sure where, but it feels good.

Drip, drip. No, go back, go back. It was good.

Drip, drip. I have woken up. I look at the clock. Two fifteen. Drip.

I am in our flat in Paris. Where is that coming from? I get up. Perhaps the boiler? No, it's water dripping from the newly painted ceiling. I wake my husband. We put something out to catch the water. I was pretty sure that the flat upstairs was empty – it is owned by a man who lives elsewhere and the tenant had left recently. We go upstairs and knock on the door. No response. Nothing to do but go back to bed.

This is known as a *dégât des eaux*. Not a phrase you learn at school. Nothing to do with the famous painter. It just means water damage. It happens all the time. Twenty years before, we had bought this small flat in Paris. A reasonable size for us – three rooms, kitchen and bathroom. Not to mention a large area for putting clothes, known in French as a *cagibi*, so we call it the KGB.

Many people thought this was very romantic. A quick trip across Kent, under the Channel and *voilà*, one is in France. And Paris! "I love Paris in the springtime"; "We'll always have Paris." So many ways to celebrate the city of light.

But we learned very quickly that not everything in Paris is romantic. The new flat needed painting and someone had recommended an Algerian decorator. As soon as we had possession of our flat, we arranged for him to paint the entire place. He was working only in the evenings, as he had a day job. I showed him the button on our newly installed telephone that would take him directly to our London house. Just in case.

And, of course, three weeks after we moved in, there was a call. His French was not easy to understand, but he was clearly very agitated: *'Mme Richardson, Mme Richardson, il y a une fuite!'*. My French was not bad, but I didn't know what a *fuite* was. He explained: *'Il y a l'eau qui coule sur les murs'* (there is water running down the walls). Somehow those were all words that I knew. A *fuite* was a kind of flood, although I later discovered that the proper word is *inondation*. Burst pipes are a regular part of Paris life.

That is when I learned a whole new vocabulary. A boiler is a *chaudière*. An estimate is a *'devis'*. The problem (leak or whatever) is the *'sinistre'*. A wonderful word in the circumstances. And, my favourite, the form you need to fill in for the insurance company (but it is a standard form) is the *'constat amiable'*, which Google translates as 'friendly report', as if neighbours with water damage were never cross with each other. Not to mention *dégâts des eaux*.

That first one was probably the worst. I had called a French friend who lived nearby, who went there immediately. He said there were two inches of water all over our apartment. The upstairs boiler had burst, probably in the morning, and water had been pouring steadily into our apartment all day. The then tenant had not come back until the evening, later than our painter. As a touch of irony that would not work in a novel, their boiler was due to be serviced the next day.

There have been seven or more *dégâts des eaux* from upstairs since then. The bath over-flowed. The pipes were leaking. A broken dishwasher was leaking. We have experienced them all. And every time, both parties must fill in paperwork for the insurance and the property managers, we then have to wait many months for the water to dry and eventually it is all put right. I certainly know the drill.

But somehow I had thought we should be OK for a few years. It had been only a month since the whole kitchen and bathroom had been re-painted after the last one. But it was not to be.

It is lovely fun to have a flat in Paris. We have gained much from the experience. But it is not always romantic.

Drip.

Postscript. This story did not end here. Although the landlord thought he had fixed the problem, it turned out he hadn't. And then the tenants' dishwasher turned out to be leaking, resulting in further flooding. A plumber supposedly sorted that out. Yet as I write, following a recent inspection, the walls continue to be wet.

We wait.

Covid-19

2020

I don't think any of us will forget the daily statistics. We turned on the television and we learned how many people had died from Covid-19 in our country or in the world that day or that week. These numbers soon became out-of-date. I wrote an article about this when the US had over 225,000 deaths and the UK close to 45,000. I questioned how much meaning this could have for us – does 225,000 deaths mean so much more than 220,000? They are both large figures and they are both overwhelming. And they are appalling.

And then there are the individual losses. For a long time, I would ask friends whether they knew anyone who had died from the virus. Generally, they hadn't. There were a lot of deaths, but they remained a miniscule proportion of the world's population, so perhaps this wasn't surprising. And then I learned, quite by accident, that an Italian woman I knew, living in London – a wise and warm child psychoanalyst – had died early on (May 2020). This brought it home to me like nothing else, the death of one lovely person among all those numbers.

All I could think of was the terrible loss not only for her family and friends but also for her patients who relied on her for their well-being. Not to mention her students (an obituary noted she was an inspirational and insightful teacher). The circles of people affected by one person's death suddenly felt very real. And it seemed very unfair that she must have never had time to prepare herself or put her things in order. Just wiped out at a stroke.

We will all be left with many strange memories of the pandemic. The strangeness of lockdown – of having our family constantly around, of doing things on Zoom and losing all the ordinary things we did in life from lunch with friends to going to the dentist. But for me, one of the most notable will be how much time we all had on our hands. For most of our lives, we had never had enough. We had struggled with children and jobs and housework and thought, "if only I had more time, I would get on with..." whatever it is we hoped to do. Even for those of us in our older years, days had seemed to disappear in our involvement with grandchildren or volunteer work or other activities. This was certainly true for me.

But suddenly most of us were presented with vast stretches of time, since the widespread lockdowns meant we were unable to do the things we used to do. In my own case, we could not visit the grandchildren, never mind friends, we could not travel – we could not even get out for long. We were all told to stay at home and keep healthy.

But did we do all these things we had always meant to do? I cannot know, but I do know in my own situation, my initial answer was a definite no. I did not clean out the attic or sort out old books. I did not take up a new language, a recommended means of improving our memories. Most of all – and very surprisingly – I found that I couldn't write. This was disturbing, indeed.

I began to wonder where my time was going. We watched the news a lot, we spent time on explicit exercise, since the never-thought-about exercise implicit in day-to-day life no longer happened, we phoned up our friends and had long chats. We tried to read or undertake other pastimes to keep our minds occupied. And it was the same the next day, with different permutations. Ground Hog Day, as several people observed. No time for getting on with all those plans.

But time was not really the issue. The real problem was our state of mind. We were restless, we couldn't settle. We worried about vulnerable relatives. We worried about the impact of the economic changes on our financial situation, not to mention that of our children and their families. Our emotions were constantly running high, our minds lacked any clarity and it was no time for getting things done. There was always tomorrow.

The writer in me found this enormously frustrating. I wanted to use my time wisely and suddenly I was frittering it away. Normally, I was highly self-disciplined, able to negotiate the family and other distractions around me, to get down to work. I could put on invisible blinkers to get myself in the right frame of mind to push out the words. But all this had disappeared. The words would not come.

Early on, I posted a short note on two separate Facebook groups for writers, saying I had found it difficult to write and how annoying I found this. I expected five or ten replies, perhaps, from each site. In fact, there were well over 200 replies from writers all over the world, almost all describing their inability to settle. And hating it. At least I wasn't alone.

And then a strange thing happened. I was so moved by the number of people in the same situation that I put together a short article on the subject for my fellow writers. I wrote another, more general, article for a broader readership. Both were very well received by readers, who said they experienced the same difficulties. And then I realised that the process of doing this had obviated the problem. I could write after all.

And this book is the result.

CONCLUDING THOUGHTS: WOULD WE LIKE TO BE YOUNG AGAIN?

They tell you, when giving a speech, that you should tell people what you are going to say, say it and then tell them again what you have said. So, following this sage advice in this very different context, I shall state once again that I find being old to be not only not bad – but indeed, it can be loads of fun. Yes, a few wheels fall off from time to time, but altogether, it feels a good time to be alive.

But let me pause for a moment and consider the converse proposition i.e. would I like to return to my past years? Do I somehow feel I was happier then? Was it easier then? Would I, in short, prefer to be young again? And, if so, how young? And what do others think?

Some people say that childhood represents the happiest years, when we are completely carefree and responsible for nothing much at all. Circumstances differ, of course, but for most people it is said to be a time when we simply have to get up in the morning, get ourselves to school, play with our friends and, perhaps, do the odd chore.

Personally, I think childhood is greatly over-rated. For some, it may have been an easy and enjoyable time, but it can also be a time of great stress. You don't understand the world, you don't know where you are going in life, your 'friends' can be difficult and sometimes even bullies. Worst of all, you don't understand yourself – neither your strengths nor your weaknesses. Some people look back and see only the positive. But I had a fair number of problems myself with childhood and watched as the same arose for my children and grandchildren in turn. I would not go back to childhood for the world.

Moving forward, becoming a teenager is undoubtedly exciting, as you begin to explore the wider world and its possibilities. You become much more aware of other people, as well as yourself and your place among your friends and others. You begin to wonder where you are heading in life and what you need to do to get there. Perhaps you feel very popular and self-confident, but I suspect this is true for only a minority. Adolescence and its aftermath represent a time of such angst that it is hard to think that many people would want to go back there.

Once you are past the worst of adolescence, life does become a little easier. You have begun to settle into a profession or job of some kind. You are exploring personal relationships, perhaps choosing a partner and having children. You may have moved to a new area because of your job or relationships. Yes, it is exciting. A lot of new joys. A new partner or husband. A new baby or two. Gaining new responsibilities at work. Beginning to get a sense of yourself. Yes, yes, yes. But as I look back, I also see a lot of problems.

The period of one's twenties is particularly problematic. You are officially declared to be an adult, but frequently don't feel or act like one. It's not easy to find a permanent place to live and, indeed, many these days continue to live with their parents. More difficult still, a lot of people feel the pressures of not really knowing where they are heading in terms of a career or even partner. If they have chosen something to do, they wonder whether they will be good enough. Some may also question whether their chosen partner is, in fact, the right one. For many, it is again an unsettling time.

It all becomes a bit easier in your thirties. Some issues have clarified themselves for good or ill. But you see yourself approaching the big 40 and wonder whether you have done well enough. And everyone is absurdly busy and pulled in many directions – the search for promotion, the needs of the partner and kids. Often, people find that even their friends are too busy to talk. Is that so great?

At least by the time people are in their 'middle years', they know themselves reasonably well. They have begun to learn how to pursue their strengths and to live with their limitations. Women have finished having all the children they will ever have, which may be seen as a joy or a relief or the source of considerable unhappiness. But we do know where we are in this respect. They may also be coping with menopausal symptoms, which may be no difficulty at all or be the cause of major problems. And they may be faced with the famous twin pressures of adolescent children and ageing parents, both of whom need their attention. For some, this can be the most stressful period of their lives.

These are all very individual matters, which vary with the trajectory of any one person's life and that of those around them. But in my own view, the older we become, the better it gets. The early years are hard, the middle ones somewhat better. The fifties were great, the sixties were just fine and the seventies have not gone downhill or at least not much. Not everyone will agree. A lot will depend on the luck of good health and good relationships, neither fully under our control. And, of course, if we could be an earlier age with the confidence and wisdom we have now, the answers would be different. But that would be cheating.

I published an article exploring this issue on two occasions, 18 months apart, on the online women's magazine, SixtyandMe.com, with readers invited to comment. Together, there were roughly 215 readers' comments. Of these, 122 expressed a clear preference for a particular age, with the following responses:

childhood:	2
teens	5
twenties:	9
thirties:	20
forties	27
fifties	8
sixties & over	51
	122 responses

In sum, 71 people (58%) indicated that they would prefer to be younger, while 51 (42%) were very happy where they were. Most of the latter were in their sixties but a small number were older, including one or two in their eighties.

This was not a random sample, but I thought it was interesting nonetheless. Although the majority said they would prefer to be younger, many of the comments were more nuanced than the simple numbers suggest. Many noted they would like to be younger, but with the knowledge and confidence that they have now, so perhaps they should really be excluded from the count. Some simply wanted to enjoy their children's childhoods all over again. And some would like to be younger to enable them to make different and better decisions about their life. In other words, this was not such a clear vote for being younger per se.

And there were a great number of satisfied older people, who were keen to explain why. Some just seemed to feel very settled with their lives:

> "For me, being 60 is perfect. I realise we all have our stories and our season. I believe my season is 60 and I intend to enjoy it." (Karen)

> "I love, LOVE the age I am now. At almost 65, I'm active, wiser, making better life choices and loving retirement." (Debra)

> "I would not want to look or be younger. My age, grey hair and wrinkles are perfect!" (Barbara)

Some talked of seeing their later years as a natural progression:

"Love being 67. I worked hard to get here happy and healthy – planning to retire in a few months and enjoy the next season of life." (Carrie)

"I am just fine with the age that I am, 67. I have had a colourful, eventful, heart-breaking, rewarding and amazing life so far. I wouldn't change a thing." (Shelly)

"I would like my body to be young, sans the creaking, the loss of strength and perhaps a few wrinkles, but I prefer to be the fine wine aged to perfection that I have become." (Carmela)

"I quite like myself at age 86. Every year has more to offer and we never know what the future has in store." (Brenda)

And some welcomed their much greater self-esteem:

"No, I wouldn't want to be younger. It took me a long time to get where I am mentally, emotionally, physically and spiritually. I would never go back. Love my life at 66." (Judi)

"It has taken me 62 years to truly start loving myself and be excited about my plans for the future...It is my time now and it is all good." (Patricia)

"Good gosh, NO. My younger life was a mess, thanks to me. Older and hopefully wiser. I have no desire to go back." (Lee)

"I'm finally figuring myself out. Why would I want to go backwards?" (Dianne)

These comments accord with a number of surveys undertaken to examine happiness at different ages. To list just one, a major study of 300,000 adults across the UK found that life satisfaction, happiness and a general feeling that life was worthwhile peaked among men and women aged 65-79 (Office for National Statistics, *Measuring National Well-being in the UK*, 2016). These feelings did drop off among those over the age of 80, however, possibly arising from poorer health and greater loneliness.

So what can we conclude from all these views? Every life has its own particular course – its peaks and troughs, its joys and tribulations. Whether the total adds up to a happy life or a disappointed one cannot be predicted in advance, arising from so many differing events over the course of our years. But it does seem that a lot of us do come to the view – taking the bad with the good – that being older has much to recommend it. It is not inevitably a difficult time. There is much left to sample, roll around our mouths and savour. In the words of one of these women – "a fine wine aged to perfection." This is a cause for celebration.

EPILOGUE: The Sting in the Tail

What do you do if you have written a whole book about being old and lucky and then you aren't? My only solution is to write about it.

By the time you are in your mid-70s and there has been no major health crisis, you know you have been lucky. If you have a spouse or partner and 'you' means both of you, you know you have been doubly lucky. Now aged 79 and my husband aged 80, I have been saying to friends for a few years that we could reasonably expect a block of concrete to fall on our heads, metaphorically speaking, at any time. No certainty of when or where, but it is definitely getting more possible.

Cancer? Heart attack? A nasty fall? Or, worse, some form of dementia?

And then that block did fall. This year, on Easter Friday evening, we were chatting about nothing in particular when my husband said that his eyes were blurry. It had just happened, there were no other symptoms, but it didn't feel right. Phone calls to a medical helpline and to an optometrist friend both elicited the suggestion he should get to an eye doctor. Both suggested a particular eye hospital, but neither hinted of any emergency.

The following day, Easter Saturday, not much was open. Even in the great metropolis that is London. Not our own GP surgery. Not the recommended eye hospital. The local optician had no appointments, but there was no eye doctor there in any case. In brief, we went to the best-known eye hospital in London, where a perceptive doctor feared it might be a stroke. To my eternal gratitude, with persistence, he obtained a referral to an excellent stroke unit in a convenient hospital.

We learned then that my husband had had a haemorrhagic stroke, resulting in an eye condition called a homonymous hemianopia. Difficult to spell H's seemed to be part of the condition. He stayed in the hospital for two nights (it should have been more, but he managed to talk himself home on the grounds that he would recover quicker with good sleep and good food – and perhaps they needed the bed).

The aftercare from the National Health Service (NHS) was brilliant. The day after he arrived home, an occupational therapist came to our home to assess his needs and provide advice. The stroke doctor phoned twice within the first two weeks, a senior stroke nurse phoned once to provide a helpline number and the senior doctor from the eye hospital also phoned to say they would be in touch when his eyes had settled down.

As for the patient, he was left very tired and with no disability except to his eyes. Indeed, after a few days, it was clear that he could read a newspaper slowly, go for walks and do most things. He could watch television, but with occasional difficulty (for instance, at times he couldn't see the football in a televised match, depending on the camera angle). But he is an avid reader, and it is likely he will be unable to read books because the slow reading means he cannot absorb the rhythm and meaning of such prose. Yes, there are audio books, but they are not the same at all.

But all of the above is a preamble to what I most want to write about, namely our reaction to the situation, particularly my own. You never know until it happens. OK, a block of concrete had fallen. Yes, this was likely to change the texture of my husband's life and therefore my own. It could, indeed, shorten his life span. We were told his eyesight might improve, but it was not likely to.

Many people become frustrated and angry in this kind of situation and I was, indeed, warned that he might undergo a personality change. That was the most terrifying suggestion of the whole experience. But he is a calm and patient man and has never expressed any frustration at all. "It is what it is," he says, "I will learn to deal with it." He has a wicked sense of humour and it has not disappeared, thank goodness. Indeed, there is no personality change at all.

I went into a period of suspended emotion – not cross, not relieved, just holding in there. Part of me certainly wanted to fall apart. To rant that this had happened and was in some way unfair. Only I knew it wasn't 'unfair' because fairness has nothing to do with these events. And my strongest reaction was that he – and therefore I – had been lucky. He could have been permanently disabled. He could have lost his speech. He could have died. But all he had was a loss of some sight. He had got off lightly, dodged the bullet, take your metaphor of choice.

At some point, roughly two weeks after the event, I did break down and have a short but powerful weep following an exploration of whether this shortened his expected life span. A terrifying chasm opened up just briefly – enough to peer over the edge – and then closed again. I think the psyche knows exactly how much pain you can take – and when – and doles it out appropriately. I went back to a sense of calm.

I think it is quite a common reaction to disasters of whatever kind to decide that you have essentially been lucky, that there is someone worse off than you. Years ago, my husband's late aunt, then widowed and in her late 70s, was flooded out of her much-loved bungalow by a major flood in North Wales. Because of sanitation issues, she was required to live in a caravan next to her house for months while the authorities slowly cleaned up the numerous houses similarly affected. It was cramped, there were limited cooking and washing facilities and it was clearly not the way she wanted to live.

Did she complain? No, she told us she felt sorry for the man down the road, who was in the same situation but with a heart condition. "It must be *really* hard for him," she noted. I thought then – and I still think now – that there is always "a man down the road." Someone worse off. Makes us appreciate what we have.

As for the future, we will continue to wait to see if there is improvement. And what resources are available for the condition. And, in the meantime, that block of concrete can still come – cancer, heart attack, a nasty fall, or, worse, some form of dementia. You just never know.

And I still prefer being old – as long as I am also healthy and extremely lucky.

Acknowledgements

As with all writers, thanks are due to numerous people who helped, like midwives, to usher this book into existence.

First, I am especially grateful to Greg Thompson who is a book editor with a difference. He did not edit any of my writing, but by pressing me with lots of questions, somehow magically helped me to find the current structure of the book. This proved all important to the final version.

Second, a number of people read and commented on early versions – in some cases, twice. These are, in alphabetical order, Matt Crisci, Patricia Gitt, Bonnie Milani, Cathy Nicholls, Nicola Rossi, and Wendy Sykes. I wish I could say that I followed their advice faithfully, but that proved to be impossible. Many of their well-thought-out recommendations regrettably contradicted each other and I was left to weigh their respective views myself. Nonetheless, they forced me to think twice, which is always a good thing to do.

Third, some of these writings first appeared on SixtyandMe.com, a major online magazine for older women, although most have been changed somewhat since then. One or two were first published by BooksGoSocial.com, a book marketing organisation for writers. One piece (an Encounter in Rome) won first prize on a blogger's monthly short story writing contest and was subsequently published in an anthology of such stories. I am very grateful to all of these people for encouraging my efforts.

Finally, I am enormously grateful to Bobby Clennell, who took time out of her busy schedule to produce the drawing for the cover. Readers may have guessed, but it is, indeed, of me.

Dear Reader

I very much hope that you liked reading this book. If you did, it would be lovely if you could write a short review on any relevant book review page. Writing a review will help other people to know whether they want to read it themselves.

It does not need to be long - even a couple of sentences is fine.

And thank you for doing so.

Note if you liked this book, you might enjoy receiving my free Substack newsletter with one short article once a fortnight.

The articles are on any subject that captures my interest. There is even one with a short video of me standing on my head.

Why not give it a try – subscribe (free): https://arichardson.substack.com/

About the author

I live in London with my husband of sixty years. I am the mother of two grown up children and have two grandsons.

Throughout my working life, I was a social researcher, exploring people's views on health and social care issues via interviews and focus groups. Because of this work, I have written numerous publications over the years addressed to both academic and professional audiences.

But my real love is writing books for general readers about people's experiences and feelings on an issue of importance to them, told in their own words.

I have written three such books, described briefly below.

If you want to learn more about me or my books, please do visit my website: www.annrichardson.co.uk.

You will find there is a short 'taster' booklet, where you can read some small parts of each book. This is called 'In Their Own Words' and can be downloaded free of charge.

Life in a Hospice: Reflections on caring for the dying,
Glenmore Press, 2017
Foreword by Tony Benn.

Dying – it's an uncomfortable topic. None of us likes to think about what our last days will be like. But if we do, we want them to be full of peace and tranquillity, with the chance to say proper goodbyes to those we love. Life in a Hospice takes you behind the scenes in end-of-life care, where you will see the enormous efforts of nurses, doctors, chaplains and others - even a thoughtful cook - to provide the calm that we all hope for.

Perhaps you are looking for end-of-life care for someone you love. Perhaps you are wondering if this is the job for you. Or you just feel like being inspired by humanity at its best. This book will be for you.

Highly Commended by the British Medical Association, 2008

"An easy-to-read book, which will surprise many readers with its lightness of touch, humanity and refreshing tone." **Dr Nansi-Wynne Evans, GP, BMA Medical Book Competition**

"The simple reflections on complex areas of care resonate long after you have finished reading the book." **Royal College of Nursing**

"Written with a clarity and sensitivity that make the book a pleasure to read. Some passages made me cry and, rather to my surprise, others made me laugh. In spite of its subject, it is a book that is full of life. It is honest and interesting. A fascinating read." **Dr Elizabeth Lee, GP**

available in paperback and e-book

translated into French and Portuguese

link: https://www.books2read.com/u/bpWk0z

Wise Before their Time: People with AIDS and HIV talk about their lives
Glenmore Press, 2017 (with Dietmar Bolle)
Foreword by Sir Ian McKellen

They are young and they have a life-threatening disease…

The year is 1991. Diagnoses of HIV are rising and there is no cure in sight. Coming from all corners of the world, over forty young men and women talk about living with HIV and AIDS. They must cope with the enormous stigma, blame and guilt associated with the disease. And there are challenges in telling their parents and partners, trying to keep healthy and looking for work – all while facing an inevitably shortened future.

Yet they remain committed to celebrating the joys of life as much as they can. The book is testimony to the resilience of the human spirit.

"This collection of true stories is as powerful as any great classic of fiction. Everyone who reads Wise Before Their Time will come face to face with the greatest challenge of our age." Sir Ian McKellen

Available in paperback and e-book

Translated into Spanish and Portuguese

link: https://www.books2read.com/u/3GYq8r

Celebrating Grandmothers: Grandmothers talk about their lives
Glenmore Press, 2017

Becoming a grandmother is both exciting and challenging. In this book, 27 women describe – in their own words – how they responded to the many new pleasures and demands of being a grandmother. You will read about how their new role changed the texture of their lives, their family relationships and their sense of themselves.

Whether you find that being a grandmother is a source of great joy – or of some pain due to sheer distance or family problems – it will speak to you. And you will gain many good ideas about how to do the best for both your adult children and your grandchildren.

'A fascinating analysis of what it feels like to be a grandmother today – from the joy and fulfilment to the disappointments and anxieties. A book to warm your heart about being a grandparent...' **Virginia Ironside, agony aunt and novelist**

This book makes an original present for new and experienced grandmothers alike.

Available in paperback and e-book

Translated into Spanish and Portuguese

Link: https://smarturl.it/celebratingrandm